CW01329521

The Yacht Guru's Bible

The Service Manual for Every Yacht

Second Edition

Alene Keenan

The Yacht Stew Guru

THE YACHT STEW GURU'S BIBLE Copyright © 2015 by the International Institute of Service Arts / Yacht Stew Solutions.

All rights reserved. No part of this document may be reproduced or transmitted in any form without written, dated, and signed permission.

ISBN-13: 978-1523651146
ISBN-10: 1523651148

Please direct any comments, suggestions or questions to:
services@yachtstewsolutions.com or twitter.com/alenekeenan

Please visit us on Facebook.com at:
http://www.facebook.com/yachtstewsolutions

Table of Contents

Preface	v
Introduction	vii
Chapter 1 - Who Do We Serve?	1
Chapter 2 - The Yacht Stew	14
Chapter 3 – Training Requirements	35
Chapter 4 – Guest Services: Formal and Informal Dining	51
Chapter 5 - Guest Services: Wine and Spirits	57
Chapter 6 - Guest Services: Coffee and Tea	90
Chapter 7 - Guest Services: Cheese, Caviar, and Cigars	111
Chapter 8 - Food Safety	125
Chapter 9 – Housekeeping and Laundry	131
Chapter 10 – Floral Arrangements	168
Chapter 11 – Getting Hired	175
Appendix A - Resources and Recommended Reading	183
Appendix B - Nautical Terminology	185
Appendix C – Service Notes	195
Appendix D – Housekeeping Basics and Overview	203
Appendix E – Yacht Stew Assessments	217
Appendix F – Yacht Stew Sample Schedule and Tasks	223
Appendix G – Hiring a Stew	233

Dedication

This book is dedicated to my wonderful, kind, generous mom, who taught me everything there is to know about loving kindness; who taught me to see the good in life, to make the best of every situation; and who always told me, "A wild flower blooms where it's planted."

Margaretta Smerud Keenan

May 24, 1921 — December 5, 2012

Preface

For over 20 years, I have dedicated my life to service on private yachts. Since forming my own company, International Institute of Service Arts (IISA), I have focused on interior service and management education for staff and crew on private yachts, private jets, in hotels, and restaurants. Yachts Stew Solutions specializes in onboard stew education, team building, workshops, and seminars. Training and mentoring the next generation of service professionals is my passion.

The following is a compilation of over 20 years of lessons learned from experience in the hospitality and yachting industry. This is the book that I wish had been available when I started out in the yachting industry as a junior stewardess more than two decades ago.

Who Should Use This Book

Yacht captains who need to know and understand every aspect of the duties stews are expected to perform. Stews play a crucial role in creating satisfaction for owners and guests, who themselves have very high standards for performance of service. They look to you, the captain, to make sure those standards are met.

Crew agents who need to find and recruit the best candidates for the position—stews who fully comprehend the scope of the job and who understand the best way to do the work. The industry needs stews who will turn out to have accurately stated their abilities, and who have enough sea time and experience to handle the positions for which they are applying. Stews must be an excellent fit with the captain and owner, and it takes a good relationship with agents to find the right position for each candidate. This book will help you help them to be the best they can be.

Charter and private yacht managers who need to know that the stews employed on their yachts know how to deliver service correctly, behave as professionals, and know how to care for and maintain the interior of the yacht, as well as its precious passengers. Charter and management companies need to know that every stew who works on the yachts in their fleet delivers service at the same high standard and truly understands what superb service on board a Super Yacht is all about. Stews are the heart and soul of any yachting operation.

Yacht owners can benefit greatly from this book, as it will provide a clear explanation of what goes into providing the services that they have come to expect and deserve. Having an in-depth understanding of what the job entails will help reduce some of the hidden costs of crewing your yacht. Crew turnover and the lack of interpersonal relationships skills combine to create some of the most expensive and most frustrating problems in yachting. This book will give you the insight you need to communicate effectively with your captain and crew to address any service delivery issues you might have that will directly affect the bottom line of your yacht operation program.

Finally, this book is for people who are considering joining us in the yachting industry, or for existing stews who want to deepen their service skills in order to reap the amazing benefits yachting has to offer. Travel, money, excitement, and adventure—this business has it all. Yachting will provide you with a lifestyle and experiences that the rest of the world can only dream about.

Introduction

My name is Alene Keenan and I am a yacht stewardess. I have been traveling and serving on yachts for over twenty years and I love it! I am still serving today and in my down time I write a column for *The Triton* (a nautical newspaper for captains and crews) called Stew Cues, that shares tips for helping stews make their jobs easier and their lives more fun and rewarding. When I'm not busy working on yachts or writing, I am running my own business, the International Institute of Service Arts, with a division for educating yacht stewards and stewardesses called Yacht Stew Solutions. I specialize in educating and team building for yacht stews, both in the classroom and at sea. I also teach general business etiquette classes, hotel and restaurant service workshops, wine and bartending classes, and various business etiquette seminars for the general public.

I grew up in a small farming community in Iowa—I'm no stranger to hard work and long days!—but I am a traveler at heart. Every summer when I was a kid, Mom and Dad packed us all into the big old Volkswagen bus and we hit the road for our summer vacation excursion. We drove all over the American Midwest and the Wild West just loving the crazy, odd, and wonderful things we found there. We stopped at every roadside attraction, museum, and natural wonder. It was so much fun and so exhilarating that I knew I had to continue seeking adventure when I grew up.

When I was in my twenties I loaded up my backpack and went looking for my destiny, just like a lot of stews today, hoping to rediscover those adventurous summers I had with my family. I looked from Wyoming to Alaska, and then Scotland to the US Virgin Islands. I finally found my calling on a boat in St. Thomas. I took a job as a hostess on a 60-foot catamaran that took customers on day trips through the islands. Each day we sailed around St. Thomas and St. John and then headed to a quiet anchorage for picnic lunches and snorkeling. I fell in love with the crystal clear, coral-filled coves and I adored being in the water with the big stingrays swimming gracefully all around me. The simple joy of sharing warmth and generosity with others and seeing the delight on their faces filled me with gratitude. I knew hospitality had to be my life.

In due course I found my next job, delivering diesel engine parts to sail boats and sport fishing boats in marinas all over the Caribbean. I can't tell you how much fun it was to have a job that required traveling on ferries and small planes! Soon I was lured in by the gorgeous, majestic, gleaming white yachts tied up at the docks. I had to see what they were about and the closer I looked, the deeper my interest grew. I got to know some of the yacht captains and was eventually invited on to serve their passengers. Once on board and shipped out, I never wanted to come back to shore. It's been a magical romance: yachts, me, and serving on the sea.

Traveling throughout the yachting communities of the United States and Europe, I've come into contact with new cultures, enjoyed fabulous foods, learned new languages, had lots of fun, and made many new friends. I have been through the Panama Canal, spent time in California, Washington, Canada, Alaska, Mexico, the Caribbean, the Bahamas, Florida, Georgia, South Carolina, New Orleans, New York, Long Island, Rhode Island, Massachusetts, New Hampshire, Maine, Great Britain, Spain, France, Italy, Turkey, Holland, and Norway aboard yachts. What a life I have! I wouldn't trade it for a hundred office jobs at twice the pay.

Over these last 20 wonderful years I have found travel riches beyond compare in small towns and big cities all over the world. Yachting has allowed me to challenge myself as I enjoyed new experiences. Ultimately I found myself, I found my calling, and I found you, dear reader. I've loved it all so much I am now dedicating the rest of my life to training and mentoring the next generation of service professionals. Let's shove off together on a learning adventure on the high seas.

Allow me to show you the ropes. There has never been a better time to climb on board. There are great opportunities out there! Anyone with some hospitality experience, a pleasant personality, a willingness to support co-workers, a sense of humor, and the ability to handle the stress of the job will love this work. Working on yachts takes you around the world in style. You'll earn a great salary, too, with almost no expenses, as your room, board, meals, and uniform are covered. Great benefits, an amazing social life, international friendships, and life-changing opportunities within the framework of a highly professional industry await you on board a yacht.

There are always openings for dedicated people who are serious about a profession in hospitality or yachting, and this book will help you prepare for that vocation. I work with captains, crew agents, charter and private yacht management companies, yacht owners, and business professionals, but first and foremost, I am an advocate for stews. If you want to excel in yachting, this book will help you master that career. Anything worth doing is worth doing well, and I will teach you everything you need to learn to have a successful career in service on yachts. This book is what I've learned in 20 years of stewing, and it has helped me create value in the lives of everyone I've touched. I hope it will do the same for you!

"Following the light of the sun, we left the Old World."
—Christopher Columbus

Chapter 1

Who Do We Serve?

"Believe in doing great work." —Anonymous

I am a yacht stewardess. When I tell people about my job, they usually ask if I work on a cruise ship. I do not. I am a service worker in the yachting industry, providing high-end private service aboard vessels ranging from casual sailboats, cabin cruisers, and sport fishing boats, all the way up to luxurious motorsailers and mega yachts. What exactly do I do on the vessel? I provide impeccable food, beverage, and hospitality service above and beyond what guests might reasonably expect. I anticipate guests' needs, I am discreet, professional, personable and attentive without ever being bothersome. I travel all over the world, and I love my job.

Working on a yacht is not the same as working on a cruise ship. However, many people do not know that yachting even exists, so it is easy to see how they would assume I work for a cruise line. Although some yachts are available for charter, most are privately owned and none of them are accessible to the general public in the same way that cruise ships are.

Life as a stewardess on board a yacht at sea means being at the ready at all times, day and night. The level of service that is expected is of the highest that exists and stems from a long legacy of servants, butlers, and hosts.

The History of Service

The history of service reaches far into the past. From the household slaves of ancient Greece and Rome, to the Medieval serfs in the royal courts, there was always someone in the home who was charged with the care of the family and their assets, including the wine and alcohol. These beverages were expensive and represented considerable private investments. The person assigned to their care and service was usually a trusted slave or a freeman who had inherited the trade. He was called a "boteler" or "bouteillier." Eventually, the European term "butler" emerged. A butler was a respected senior male member of a household staff, who was in charge of a strict service hierarchy.

During Elizabethan and Victorian times, the number of butlers and other domestic servants increased in many countries, including America. From the beginnings of slavery in the United States in 1676, African-Americans were forced to serve as domestic servants. European indentured servants formed another group of domestic workers in America. Like the slaves, these servants had not volunteered for domestic service; they were forced into it by indebtedness or coercion. Qualified workers moved up through the ranks of both groups and became butlers.

Fast forward 236 years to 1912 and the glory days of transatlantic steamship travel. When we think about service on a luxurious ocean-going vessel, no grander image comes to mind than that of the ill-fated *Titanic*, making her maiden voyage from Southampton en route to the United States. Designed to be the last word in comfort and extravagance, the ship was fitted with the highest level of luxury for the time, including an on-board gymnasium, plunge pool, libraries, high-class restaurants, and sumptuous cabins.

In 1912 anyone who lived in an American or European aristocratic family would expect to be treated in high esteem. One can only imagine what it must have been like on the ship, as staff tended to the well-to-do passengers' every whim. Clearly, many of the luxuries of wealth and affluence were the same then as they are now, and involved scandalous, ostentatious behavior along with extravagance and elegance.

The formalities of service in the early 1900's give us insight into the giver and receiver relationship of service today. For the staff of the Titanic, the decision to serve was probably the result of an economic need and social station, rather than a vocational choice, as it is today. The ship's tragic demise epitomized the end of an era, reflecting the rituals of service as they were passed from the Old World to the New.

Change was in the air at the turn of the century. Between the sinking of the Titanic in 1912 and the end of the Great War, World War I (1914-1918), major adjustments in European and American society came about. During the war, young men from every social class and station were called to duty. Not only were they threatened with the loss of life or limb, but also with the very real loss of their place in society. For the European upper classes, the demise of nearly an entire generation of young men, many of them heirs to great titles and estates, struck a blow at the foundation of the class system

With the resulting changes in society, autonomy and independence were thrust upon women, whether they wanted it or not. Both in Europe and in America, female employees no longer needed the security of domestic service when they could work in munitions factories. The servility required of them became obsolete, and the numbers employed in domestic service fell sharply.

The domestic service industry lay dormant for many years. Today, it seems that the elaborate rules of service from the days of the Titanic have vanished forever, but really, it's the servile mentality that's gone. Service today has evolved in proportion to people's ever changing needs for comfort and just as importantly, for privacy. Along the way, the expectancies and attitudes of service have shifted away from one of "hired domestics" to that of acknowledged professionals who are more essential than ever. These days, it is generally recognized that service is an art form that requires expertise.

Who We Serve

"We all have the power to give away love, to love other people. And if we do so, we change the kind of person we are, and we change the kind of world we live in."
—Harold Kushner

Today's world has many different examples of high net-worth individuals and celebrity personality types. They often have vast estates, yachts, and private aircraft that demand precise management skills, technical knowledge, and awareness of professional service relationships. Managing these environments is really about managing a particular lifestyle and quality of life and the service abilities needed are much more than simply housekeeping and ironing skills. Today's professionals have cutting-edge knowledge of event planning, etiquette, fine dining and wine, jewelry, expensive clothing, collectibles, computer literacy, technology, security, safety, and much, much more.

One of the biggest challenges is that sometimes our employers require a high level of privacy and security; consequently, we may know very little about them. A personal assistant or owner's rep may give us some information, and there may be a basic outline available listing likes and dislikes regarding food, beverages, and personal favorites. As for charter guests, the charter broker will give them a preference sheet that they send back, which should outline dietary restrictions and preferences, but typically there isn't a lot of information provided (See page 208 for more sample sheets). Therefore, we frequently have to figure it out on our own based on trial and error.

For example, one owner I worked for conducted a lot of business entertaining onboard. I normally served meals to him once or twice a month. He always greeted me by name and was always very gracious and polite, but he was a man of few words and most of our communication was just eye contact. He would give me a look and from that I would figure things out such as: how much time does he have for this meal; how fast does he want the courses to come out; or, if he's in a hurry, should I wait until all the guests have finished eating before I clear courses, or should I clear each plate as people finish? After the meal service, he would stop by the pantry and look me straight in the eye and say thank you. He rarely said much to us, but his secretary would call and thank us and share any comments he had made to her about the meal and the service.

On the other hand, I worked for one family for several years and they were very open and friendly with me. I knew nearly everything about them, but they knew almost nothing personal about me. We were very fond of one another and often laughed and joked together, yet we maintained very strict professional boundaries.

Other owners and guests that I have worked with preferred a more casual relationship. Service was more informal and the evenings would include games and singing karaoke together.

You just never know how the service relationship is going to unfold. Believe me, there is always, always, always a way to make it wonderful for the guests. In the beginning, I would suggest that you set the standard very high, gauge their reaction, and adjust boundaries accordingly. It's possible to maintain formality while still creating a fun atmosphere. It's important to note that you must follow any rules that prohibit drinking alcohol with or around your guests, whether you are on or off duty. It is essential to maintain a professional image. Being a good person is good business.

Service Standards and Expectations

Service onboard yachts is at the owner's or guest's request and it is assumed that stews will have the right combination of skills to do the job. For example, stews must be able to set the table and serve both formal and informal meals, know how to mix cocktails, and have a solid basic knowledge of wine and how to serve it.

As a yacht stew, you will have to deliver service in a formal style setting, so a basic knowledge of everyday etiquette and an understanding of international and business protocol are essential. *Kiss, Bow, or Shake Hand* by Terri Morrison and Wayne A. Conaway is an excellent source of information on international courtesy and protocol. It gives insight into requirements for serving guests of many nationalities, as well as into relationships with crew members from different nations.

Webster's dictionary defines service as "to answer the needs of, and provide assistance that benefits, others."

There are many levels of service performed in our economy every day, from the person who waits on you at the coffee shop in the morning to the person who cleans that coffee shop at night; from the firemen and policemen who protect our communities to the person in customer service you speak with to get technical support or voice a complaint.

Within each of these examples are various levels of accountability. Each of us has our own internal set of values and expectations regarding customer service, and our requests are not always met the way we would like them to be. Face-to-face customer service, along with good food service in many restaurants, has practically disappeared. One has to wonder what direction service in general is taking these days.

But when you work on a yacht, you are all about service, so consider this: the *highest* level of service is service within a private living environment, and the level of service performed on a yacht is often the highest level of all. As a yacht steward or stewardess, we serve in what is known as the "luxury market" which is characterized by wealth and sophistication. The ultimate environment, combining the owner's vision, design, and lifestyle concepts, is created aboard luxurious mega yachts. The highest level of service imaginable takes place here.

Your function as a yacht stew is to provide service to the owners and guests while onboard. It is also your job to coordinate the many aspects of the job, including the various duties that entail taking care of the crew. It's up to stews to ensure that the departments interact seamlessly and that our own work is invisible and appears effortless.

To be entrusted with a person's private life, belongings, family, guests, and personal affairs requires a substantial amount of trust. Without a doubt, it is an honor as well as a responsibility. Yacht stews help create order, dignity, and a sense of peace. That is a powerful and valuable contribution. In a nutshell, stews are the glue that holds the whole program together.

We set the tone for others with our ability to remain unruffled in stressful situations. We must appear cool and collected, even when things are melting down around us. Our compassion and exceptional communication skills can help crew members who are at odds with each other to talk things out. Our insight can resolve a potentially risky situation.

A life in service is the highest possible calling. Service is not submission; it is a finely tuned set of skills. The work yacht stews do in a private service environment adds value and enriches the lives of the owners and their guests. By agreeing to serve, we agree to follow someone else's agenda, and to do so with an open heart. As Gandhi said, "The best way to find yourself is to lose yourself in service to others."

Types of Yachting

It is important to understand the demographics of yachting. First of all, there are different categories: commercial, private, or a combination of the two. Different laws apply to each, and they are set up somewhat differently. Within each category of commercial or private, we have various modes of operation. For instance, if the yacht is docked in a marina and no guests onboard, the daily routine and schedule will be simpler than if there are owners or guests onboard (See Appendix F). In the first case, it will be a basic 8-5 routine that will consist mostly of cleaning, maintenance, and regularly scheduled tasks. There will be daily, weekly, and monthly checklists. Unless you are the designated watch person, you will most likely be off duty for the evening depending on the location, the captain, and the standing orders of the vessel.

If there are owners or charter guests onboard, the crew will be "in service" and most likely on call or on duty 24/7. A detailed schedule that covers every moment of the day, from the time that guests get up until the time that they go to sleep will be in place. The crew will have designated hours of work and break times. You may or may not be allowed to leave the vessel during your break or when you are not on duty. When you are "in service" you are expected to make your work your focus and to complete all of the tasks that are assigned to you.

If the yacht is in transit, the mode of operation will vary depending on whether or not there are guests onboard, whether the yacht is simply moving from one port to the next, and whether the trip will be several hours or several days or more. A vessel always has to be stowed for travel, meaning anything that could move or fall or be damaged or cause damage has to be set down in a safe spot. This can include taking pictures and art work off of the walls and securing items and furniture depending on the sea conditions. When there are guests on, it is usually only for a short journey and the service routine is adjusted to fit the circumstances. If the yacht is doing a crossing it could take several days or weeks and the schedule and routines are adjusted drastically. Owners and guests are rarely onboard for crossings.

When the yacht is in a shipyard it is in another mode of operation. For some reason a number of people are under the impression that if the ship is in the yard, there is nothing for the crew to do. On the contrary, this is the time for large maintenance and repair projects. The crew will be directly involved in the progress of these projects, often working with subcontractors directly and being in charge of maintaining the work areas and ensuring the safety and security of all interior furnishings and décor. It is crucial to inspect and clean regularly when there are workers onboard. In some cases this is the time of year when crew will rotate out for vacation or training.

Yacht Size Classification

The word "yacht" is derived from the Dutch word "jacht," which means "hunt." It was originally defined as a light, fast sailing vessel used by the Dutch navy to pursue pirates and other transgressors around and into the shallow waters of the "low countries."

People often ask what the difference is between a yacht, a boat, and a ship. Generally speaking a yacht is a vessel used for pleasure purposes, while a ship is a vessel used for commercial purposes. Another expression that is often used is that a boat will fit inside a ship, but a ship will not fit inside a boat.

Yachts can range in their overall length (Length Over All or LOA) from about 40 feet to well over 300 feet, where the distinction between a yacht and a ship becomes blurred. The cost of building and keeping a yacht rises quickly as length increases.

The Chain of Command

On all yachts, there is a "chain of command" through which authority is granted and grievances are addressed. It is important to know what that chain of command is and to follow professional protocol. It is considered unprofessional to overstep your professional boundaries and may be considered insubordination. The crew required to operate a large or super luxury yacht can number anywhere from eight members for a 120-foot yacht, to a complement of 70+ members for a 500-foot yacht.

A typical crew consists of three departments: the deck, the interior, and the engineering department. Within the deck department are the Captain, First Officer, Deck Officers and Deck Hands. The engineering department will include the Chief Engineer, Second and Third Engineer, and IT Engineer(s). The interior consists of Chef(s) and Sous Chef(s), and the Chief, 2nd and Junior Stews. Larger yachts will have a Purser, Head of Service, and Head of Housekeeping. Often there will be a Chief Steward who deals closely with the owner, acting as a sort of Butler/Valet/Personal Assistant.

Captain or Commanding Officer (CO)

The Captain is responsible for the safety of the ship; the overall success of the trip; the efficiency of operation; the wellbeing, comfort, and morale of all embarked personnel; and all property and equipment assigned to the ship. The Captain's authority extends over all embarked personnel at all times aboard ship, in the ship's launches, or on duty ashore. All personnel must follow any lawful order of the Captain.

The Captain answers either to the yacht owner or its management company. He is in charge of navigation and operation of the vessel, standards of seamanship and safety, human resources, finances, the seaworthiness of the vessel, and crew training requirements.

The Captain wears 4 gold bars with an anchor emblem on his shoulder epaulets or jacket sleeves when in dress uniform.

While the formality associated with good order and discipline should be followed in all conduct aboard ship, the Captain is always available and may be approached by anyone for the resolution of issues.

[Image courtesy of Big Blue Yachtwear]

Executive Officer (XO), First Officer, or Chief Mate

The XO is second-in-command and takes overall responsibility for the operating conditions of the ship. The XO is also tasked with budgetary and policy matters, is responsible for the medical operations, and in the absence of the Captain, assumes command of the ship. He is responsible for management of the crew, the deck department, and the navigation of the vessel and will assist the Captain with onboard training.

The XO wears 3 gold bars with an anchor emblem on his shoulder epaulets or jacket sleeves when in dress uniform.

Chief Engineer/Engineers/Electronic Technicians

The Engineering Department is responsible for the operation, maintenance and repair of all propulsion and the ship's auxiliary machinery. Engineering is responsible for the ship's electrical system, engines, ventilation, hydraulic, sanitation, and refrigeration, and for all machinery onboard. The department is also responsible for the maintenance of all the "toys," dinghies, outboard motors, tenders, and all mechanical and electrical equipment on board.

The Chief Engineer wears 4 gold bars with a propeller emblem on his shoulder epaulets or the sleeves of his dress jacket.

The Second Engineer wears 3 gold bars with a propeller emblem on his epaulets or the sleeves of his dress jacket. He will stand on engine room watch and will assist as needed in maintenance and running of the vessel. He is second in command of the engine department, answers to the Chief Engineer, and will assume the Chief Engineer's duties if that person is incapacitated or absent.

Officer of the Watch (OOW) or Bosun

The OOW or Bosun answers to the First Mate and is responsible for the general management of the deck hands. He is in charge of overseeing the care and running of all onboard "toys," such as jet skis and dinghies, and of the docking equipment and hydraulic lifts.

The OOW/Bosun wears 2 gold bars and an anchor emblem on his shoulder epaulets or the sleeves of his dress jacket.

Deck Officer and Deck Hands

Any Deck Officer is a direct representative of the Captain and is responsible for the safe navigation of the ship and the conduct of operations during an assigned watch period. A Deck Officer may be assigned personnel to assist in these duties, and these personnel are directly under the Deck Officer's supervision for the duration of the watch. They are responsible for all deck work required to run and maintain the yacht, such as sanding, varnishing, cleaning, and the launch and recovery of jets skis, dinghies, etc.

The Deck Hands wear one or more gold bar and an anchor emblem on their shoulder epaulets or the sleeves of their dress jackets.

Chef/Sous-Chef

Yacht Chefs are assigned the job of creating dishes for private yacht owners and their families and guests, as well as the crew. This requires a menu of three meals a day, seven days a week. Galley cleaning, menu planning, and selecting and organizing provisions are the additional responsibilities of a professional Chef aboard a yacht. The Chef maintains the galley and the refrigerators and freezers.

The Chef answers to the Captain and/or the Financial Officer. He wears 4 silver bars with a crossed knife and fork on his or her shoulder epaulets when in dress uniform.

[Chief Stew Donna with 3 stripes, Chef Paul with 4 stripes, and Second Stew Alene with 2 stripes]

Chief Stew/Purser
Second/Junior Stews

The Chief Stew/Purser is responsible for the management and appearance of the yacht interior, as well as looking after the needs and requirements of the guests and managing the Interior Crew. Duties involve overseeing all interior spaces, including living quarters, dining areas, guest cabins/showers/baths, day heads and bars. The Chief Stew also works in conjunction with the Chef, purchasing, stowing and preparing food and looking after much of the food and beverage requirements of the owners and guests, as well as the crew. The department also maintains the crew mess area, lounges, library, laundry room, and interior storage spaces.

The Chief Steward/Stewardess or Purser wears 3 or 4 silver stripes with a crescent moon emblem on his/her shoulder epaulets in dress uniform. The Second and Junior stews wear the number of bars appropriate for their position aboard.

[Alene and crew aboard Mystique]

"Team work makes the dream work." —Anonymous

13

Chapter 2
The Yacht Stew

Numerous books have been written about the procedures and skills needed to be successful in the hotel and restaurant business. The operation of a yacht involves most of these same elements, however there are some differences, one of which is that they are carried out with a much smaller staff. On a yacht, the interior service team is responsible for several departments, including accommodations, housekeeping, and food and beverage operations. All crew members live on the yacht in very tight quarters, and are frequently "on call" 24/7 when there are guests aboard. It is important that the Chief Stew understands all aspects of housekeeping as well as service, because it is their responsibility to create and delegate the task schedule to get all daily work done in the allotted time.

The Responsibilities of a Yacht Steward/Stewardess

A yacht stew is responsible for managing and providing all necessary services within the interior areas of the yacht. First and foremost, this means giving meticulous attention to the needs of the yacht's owner(s) and their guests. It also means that you are responsible for maintaining all interior surfaces, lighting, fabrics, upholstery, carpets, appliances, TV's, equipment, laundry, bathrooms, bedrooms, galleys, holds, drawers, lockers, linens, dishes, silverware, liquor, and maybe even the kitchen sink, in a 5-star state at all times!

On a luxury yacht, the ratio of crew to owner/guests is much smaller than in any other hospitality environment (restaurant, hotel, airline, etc). This means there is a lot more one-on-one attention given to each VIP onboard.

Basic Knowledge and Skills Required:

- Basic seamanship knowledge
- Yacht departments and hierarchy
- STCW 95 Basic Safety and Security Awareness
- Self-discipline and motivation
- Awareness of etiquette, ethics, and professional boundaries
- Security, confidentiality, and privacy of guests and owners
- Communication skills
- Proper decorum, personal hygiene, appearance and attitude
- Knowledge of International Protocol and proper forms of address
- Knowledge of food service styles and cuisine
- Food safety and hygiene
- Silver Service knowledge and skills
- Set-up and order of service in formal and informal dining
- Meal serving and clearing sequence
- Caviar history and service
- Cheese service
- Entertainment and party planning skills
- Buffet, party, and picnic service
- Floral knowledge and arrangement skills
- Tea and coffee history and service
- Knowledge of wine history, characteristics, and service
- Knowledge of guest preferences, food allergies, religious observances of diet and customs
- Management of product inventories and provisioning
- Guest services and valet services
- Laundry care and procedures; care of fine, expensive fabrics and items of clothing
- Spot treatment and stain removal
- Knowledge and care of exotic furnishings; care of special finishes and upholstery fabrics
- Knowledge and care of valuable art pieces
- Care and storage of fine china, silverware, and stemware

What is Personal Service?

"The work of your heart, the work of taking time to listen, to help, is also your gift to the whole world." —Jack Kornfield

Service is an intangible product. No transfer of ownership or possession takes place when service is performed, it is instantly perishable, and cannot be stored or transported. It has an emotional aspect as well as a physical aspect and can be ambiguous in nature. Service can be broadly defined in terms ranging from time spent in military service; to the service professions, including waiters, bartenders, policemen, firemen, doctors and lawyers; to the individual who delivers your mail or repairs the transmission in your car. All agree with Webster's definition: "Meeting the needs of and providing assistance that benefits others."

In yachting, we work within a personal service environment. This service model is a cross between hotel food and beverage amenities and estate management, as carried out in a private environment. In this elite setting, service is privileged and very exclusive. For private service to succeed, there must be an exchange of information so that both giver and receiver understand their roles, and know what level and type of service is expected. Without this information, service cannot be smooth, effective, or consistent.

A good server works on developing specialized knowledge, advanced communication skills, and professional etiquette. Confidence in the ability to serve translates into high self-esteem and confidence, which create a favorable first impression for guests. Poise and self-assurance are reflected in one's body language. Nonverbal communication expresses the server's level of willingness and enthusiasm, and can convey a positive or negative feeling. Obviously, a positive state makes people feel more comfortable and puts them at ease.

Three Basic Elements for Good Service Performance

1. A defined concept of the model and standard of service

Stews are expected to determine and then exceed guests' expectations, ranging from basic amenities to lavish indulgence. A fair amount of conjecture is involved at times, so good organization and communication is critical for things to run smoothly. By being orderly and efficient in the work environment, any miscalculation and the resulting stress is kept at a manageable level.

Exceptional time management skills are crucial. The Chief Stew is responsible for creating and delegating the task schedule in order to get all daily work done in the allotted time. If scheduled tasks are not understood and smoothly carried out, "crisis mode" can come up at the worst possible moments, greatly increasing the stress level. But before they can plan routine duties, not just in service but in housekeeping as well, stews must fully comprehend the daily, weekly, and monthly task overview. Frequently, a new stew will be assigned to the housekeeping routine known as "heads and beds" for a while before being scheduled in service, so that their performance can be observed and monitored before they are promoted to guest service.

2. A common vision, protocol and etiquette standards maintained by all

A mission or vision statement for every yacht is essential for defining the level of service. Each vessel has its own social style and structure. It is a mix of the owner's dream, along with the yacht management and the captain's administration and supervision styles, combined with the day-to-day organization and housekeeping structure that bring the vision to life. Many of the tasks required in serving on board yachts are mundane and repetitive, especially when it comes to housekeeping, guest services, and social behavior, but everyone on the team needs to recognize their importance in order to support service procedures.

A protocol is a rule that guides how an activity or task should be performed. Performance standards cannot be established and tasks cannot be delegated effectively without protocols. For stews, it is important to understand the structure of personal service in addition to the food and beverage delivery system, along with the techniques of the housekeeping department

Etiquette is a code of conduct that outlines expectations for social behavior according to conventional norms within a society, class, or social group, usually involving civil virtues such as truthfulness, self-control, and kindness towards others. It changes and evolves over time, and it is culturally specific.

Etiquette plays a role in modeling crew relations too. What is acceptable in one culture may be seen as a terrible mistake in another and without meaning to, we can offend others by our behavior. A good example of this is basic table manners. Some people are appalled by the table manners of others and this basic behavior can create an underlying rift in crew relations, which is most certainly unintentional.

3. An outline of policies, processes and procedures to organize the service standards

The service model also consists of administration, housekeeping, food and beverage service, personal service, safety and security, and maintenance duties. These standards are the rules and the protocol that one is expected to follow for that particular yacht and may vary.

It is no small task to break down all of the individual elements of the service model and the criteria that are expected for each one of them. In yachting, oftentimes there will be a written manual of sorts that outlines policies, processes, and procedures on the yacht, but sometimes there won't. The service model on different yachts may cover roughly the same criteria, but the standards can be totally different.

Due to the nature of luxury service within a private environment, the stews must understand:

- The actions and tasks that are required daily, weekly, and monthly to meet the guest services requirements that fit in with the yacht's travel and maintenance schedule
- The training and skills that are needed to meet the demands of guest services, housekeeping, administration, and maintenance
- How to schedule tasks and how they are timed and spaced throughout the day
- Proficiency with tools and products needed to complete all jobs successfully in accordance with the yacht's standards and protocols. Each yacht is unique.
- How to introduce variety, intellectual challenge, and feedback; people function better and are more connected psychologically when they are given a variety of tasks to complete, when their tasks require a thinking process in order to finish their work, and when they are given regular feedback.

The New Standard: Choosing Service

"Have a heart, lend a hand, make a difference."
—Anonymous

Service is a mutually beneficial relationship that adds value to life. The act of service empowers the server while at the same time enriching the life of the receiver. It is a delicate balance of professional skills and trust. Stews must have not only the responsibility, but also the authority to carry out tasks that support service.

Service is an art form requiring self-exploration and self-assessment of personal strengths and weaknesses. It can be difficult for some people to work according to someone else's preferences and schedule, but the true "service heart" chooses to serve because service is what they want to do. Service is their vocational calling.

On the other hand, "service hearts," while excelling at fulfilling the needs of others, may have difficulty getting their own needs met and asking for help. Developing a service model requires time management supervision along with the ability to integrate management skills with service criteria. The model depends on the capacity of the stews to meet or exceed the standards of the specific yacht that they are employed by.

There are certain conditions that must be met in order for service to be successful:

- Leadership management and training is essential. Many times service professionals are non-confrontational by nature. They would prefer to serve rather than to manage and do not like intimidating situations.

- Recognition of the business side of a service lifestyle. A job description is crucial, as well as an understanding of healthy business practices and leadership abilities.

- The ability to think through requests and understand the resources available to meet the needs of guests. Stews must develop the skills to meet the needs of unusual requests and unique lifestyles – and ask for assistance when necessary.

- Clarity of purpose. Management must implement whatever tools are necessary to provide clear direction, including detailed instruction, "how to" lists, timetables, daily/weekly/monthly checklists, travel schedules, and any empirical data that facilitates success.
- Management must foster and implement high self-esteem along with appropriate personal and professional boundaries. Abusive behavior from employers, guest, or co-workers is not acceptable.
- Service relationships must be mutually satisfying to be successful. It is important to create balance in life in order to avoid burnout.

Service requires the ability to work on someone else's schedule and according to their code of expectations. Time management techniques are vital to complete all of the daily tasks on our work schedule. The sheer volume of work that is required to be completed each day often overwhelms new stews. However, knowledge of a variety of techniques and work styles can help to master this aspect of the art of service.

Service requires honest self-exploration and self-assessment of personal strengths and weaknesses. Stews must be able to individually tailor service to meet the needs of each situation while at the same time upholding common standards and expectations. Effective communication skills, the ability to negotiate and resolve conflict, and the development of appropriate boundaries are critical tools for effective service.

Management must work to create real leaders and mentors within the organization and to value and appreciate the contributions and suggestions of team members. It is important to establish a service code of ethics, etiquette and professional boundaries. Discipline must be developed to manage disagreements and dysfunctional relationships that foster negativity.

While there are many fundamental technical skills that a stew needs to master, interpersonal skills are just as important and they can be the key to success in a yachting career. Working on yachts puts you under a lot of pressure, and much of the time you will be performing your job in a less than optimal environment. You will have to juggle many demands while remaining flexible, working long hours, and sometimes functioning with very little sleep. Occasionally, you may get very frustrated and emotional, yet you have to learn to control your reactions, stay calm, and keep the larger goal in mind.

The ability to enjoy making other people happy and to anticipate their needs is a job prerequisite. It means you will be able to take care of the owners, guests, captain and crew on the vessel while always maintaining a positive, cheerful and caring attitude. Everyday manners and etiquette are important. Respect and consideration for others is key.

The secret of success is directly related to your *attitude* and the subsequent effect you have on those around you. Good communication and listening skills and strong personal and professional boundaries are fundamental. You will have to be able to work out your own emotional "stuff" and not impose personal issues upon the rest of the crew or the guests. The work can be really hard, but grumbling and complaining doesn't help matters any, and it brings everybody down.

Being a yacht stew is definitely a career where you must be willing to be a "team player" and help out in other departments. It is equally important to be able to ask for help when you need it. You will also have to overcome being judgmental when it comes to living and working with other crew members; we all have a different worldview and different interests and abilities, so it is sometimes challenging to get along.

It is helpful to remember that we all have character flaws and we will have to challenge our own limits and belief systems in order to coexist peacefully. Remember that character flaws are not the same as personality disorders; sometimes we just need to take it easy on each other and dig a little deeper inside to find compassion.

> "Believe there's a light at the end of the tunnel. Believe you might be that light for someone else."
> — from "Believe" by Dan Zadra and Kobi Yamada

Stewardess Duties

The following are two examples of standard stewardess duties when guests are not present. In the first example, imagine we're at the dock or in the shipyard. In the second, we are underway without guests.

Stewardess Duties without Guests Onboard
Docked or in a Shipyard

Every day cleaning in all areas:

- Opening duties as needed
- Check Laundry
- Clean crew mess and stock snacks and beverages
- Clean captain's cabin and office, wheelhouse and radio room
- Vacuum / Dust all surfaces, including kick plates, baseboards, air con vents, etc. in all areas
- Clean/sanitize all remotes, telephones, and touchpad surfaces
- Empty trash
- Use proper products for materials and surfaces:
    - Use diluted vinegar and water on varnished surfaces
    - Use alcohol/water on stainless appliances and fixtures; polish as needed
    - Mild soap and water or disinfectant as needed
- Check all mirrors, glass, windows for smudges
- Vacuum all floors, carpet and/or canvas covers
- Wash floors
- Launder area rugs as needed

Throughout the day:

- Be available to welcome guests/contractors and offer beverages at Captain's request
- Make sure interior surfaces are protected at all times, i.e. with contractors working or any projects that crew are involved with
- Check wheelhouse and office at end of work day for any dishes or debris
- Double check all work areas for tidiness at the end of the day
- Closing duties as needed

Once per week:

- Clean and flush all toilets; Run faucets
- Check and replace light bulbs
- Dust all surfaces in rooms, including door tops, lamps, vases, windowsills, etc.
- Polish/dust art pieces as instructed
- Check and dust or polish marble surfaces as needed
- Clean and organize all cabinets in stew pantry
- Clean and organize all cabinets in guest service areas

Once per month or more:

- Check and clean all air con vents and filters
- Polish any stainless around doors, kick plates, etc.
- Dust/clean walls in all rooms
- Vacuum under sofa cushions
- Clean and organize linen lockers for supplies and turn-down items
- Clean, organize, inventory cleaning supply lockers and under sinks

As needed:

- Wipe out all guest drawers and closets
- Wash shower curtains
- Stock guest bathrooms
- Master Stateroom:
  - Clean and organize drawers, cabinets, and closets
  - Inventory and organize toiletries
  - Clean, maintain, and organize owner shoes, clothing and personal items

- Miscellaneous:
    - Organize and inventory light bulbs and batteries
    - Check and sanitize all electronics, touchpad's and remotes as needed
    - Polish all silver, brass and other metal items
    - Clean and organize all media, game, movie, and entertainment items
    - Spot-clean or deep-clean carpet, upholstery, etc. as needed
    - Work on projects list
    - Polish all hardware, hinges, kick plates, interior stainless and metal fittings
    - Clean and maintain all ice machines, vacuum cleaners, coffee machines, small electrical tools
    - Inventory, clean, and stock all alcohol and wine items
    - Maintain cleanliness of all items and surfaces in all stew areas and pantries
    - Maintain all linens, table decorations, etc.

Stewardess Duties without Guests and Underway

- Watch duties as required
- Work underway as scheduled
- Meal service for crew
- Co-ordinate meal times and food items
- Check beverages for crew
- Put out snacks for watch duties
- Check boat every hour/ walk through all areas
- Assist with watch duties as needed if not on watch schedule
- Clean and check bridge area for cleanliness and clean as needed
- Follow rules for uniforms underway
- Follow rules for garbage and recycling
- Follow rules for behavior underway/ notify bridge if you are going outside
- NO SUNTAN OIL ON THE DECK!!!
- Help keep crew area tidy and quiet when watchmen are sleeping. Be nice.

Administrative Duties

The administrative duties for the Interior Department will vary from one yacht to the next, but at the most basic level, stews should know how to:

- Describe and understand job specifications and description
- Identify and demonstrate understanding of department procedures and guidelines
- Describe and understand the various schedules and checklists for the department
- Demonstrate and identify the requirements of inventories to be taken for the department and be able to take an inventory
- Understand and demonstrate basic accounting and bookkeeping procedures as needed
- Understand and demonstrate computer skills (Excel, Word, spreadsheets for inventories, etc.)
- Describe and understand terms of contract
- Be aware of and comply with all applicable national and international maritime laws, regulations and security mandates including flag state, customs and immigrations, USCG, STCW and MCA regulations.

Yacht Etiquette, Ethics and Privacy

"Do your little bit of good where you are; it's those little bits of good put together that overwhelm the world."
—Archbishop Desmond Tutu

The moment you are invited to step onboard a yacht, you enter the world of an elite socio-economic class and those fortunate enough to be of service to them. As such, you are being accepted as a person who understands and applies the ethical code that is relevant on that particular yacht. Etiquette may be defined generally as "the code of conduct that describes expectations for social behavior according to contemporary conventional norms within a society, social class, or group." Not every rule will be written down, but with a bit of effort you can learn to assimilate yourself into any yacht-specific rules of etiquette. Over time, you will understand that following these simple rules makes life simpler and more pleasant for everyone. It reduces the possibility of misunderstandings and creates many more opportunities for mutual respect and courtesy.

Keep in mind your own personal manners and value system. As Norman Cousins said, "Nothing is more beautiful or powerful than an individual acting out of his or her conscience, thus helping to bring the collective conscience to life."

A Brief History of Manners and Value Systems

All known literate societies have developed codes of behavior, and philosophers have been writing about ethics for thousands of years. Throughout history, elaborate systems of social rules have evolved to maintain a separation between rulers and common citizens. As class structures changed and commoners were granted more privileges, the social structure changed too. Out of necessity, guidelines to teach people how to behave properly in relation to others were created.

In America, George Washington and Benjamin Franklin wrote codes of conduct for the behavior of young gentlemen in the "new" American Colonies, even before the American Revolution. Their advice was based on rules of behavior they brought to the colonies from England, blended with new ideas brought back from the courts of Europe while in the process of seeking support for the American Revolution and building trade and political ties from 1775-1783.

Proper decorum was a major concern for Americans from the very beginning. An American author and former slave, Robert Roberts, wrote a guide in 1827 called *Robert's' Guide for Butlers and Other Household Staff* so that servants could "more proficiently perform the duties for which they were being paid." *Mrs. Beaton's Book of Household Management*, first published in 1861, was a popular tome used by many to establish guidelines to running all aspects of a household here in America as well as in Victorian England. It included numerous tips on dealing with servants, the service hierarchy and servant relationships.

Modern American writers on the topic of etiquette and proper social behavior include Emily Post and Letitia Baldrige. In the UK, Debrett's Publishing has published a range of guides on traditional British etiquette, dating from the mid 1900's, which most likely influenced the rules we adopted here.

In all cases, one's social esteem relies on what to do, or more importantly, what *not* to do, in order to be seen as a proper, polite and refined member of society. The concept of manners and etiquette are culturally dependent and therefore, what is common behavior in one culture may be absolutely appalling in another. It's important to remember also that etiquette is continuously evolving; behavior that was perfectly acceptable during one era may go out of style and no longer be considered acceptable, and vice versa.

The Top 10 Work Principles and Ethic Requirements

"Heart, instinct, principles." —Blaise Pascal

Today, organizations of all sizes adopt an ethical code for the purpose of assisting everyone within the organization to apply the principles of "right" and "wrong" to their everyday decision-making. A workplace code of ethics typically has three distinct levels: a) business ethics codes, b) codes of employee conduct, and c) codes of professional conduct.

I would like to thank Mary Louise Starkey for the inspiration for this following section. Her classic book, *"The Original Guide to Private Service Management"* contains a "Top 10" list, which I have adapted for use here.

For yacht stews, the ethics you need to know to render professional onboard services include:

- **Knowledge:** Develop the ability to visualize and establish a safe and healthy environment based on the service and housekeeping standards and expectations that have been determined for the style and level of guest service onboard the yacht. Safety and seamanship are of great concern on a yacht at all times.

- **Integrity:** Accept responsibility for maintaining strict confidence regarding personal information you may learn about your employer and guests. Always protect the privacy and safety of the owner, guests and the vessel itself; refrain from gossip; and be nonjudgmental. Yachts are very high profile and under the constant scrutiny of prying eyes and paparazzi. Proper discretion is part of a yacht security plan.

- **Character:** Have the courage and conviction to uphold the highest level of professional standards in all relationships and technical skills, whether the employer is onboard or not, and always act in the best interest of your employer. On some yachts you will be allowed to use some of the guest toys, equipment, and amenities, but do not assume that is the case. Always remember, if you break it, you bought it.

- **Service:** Treat the employer and guests consistently at the level of service that best meets their needs and desires; promote a comfortable, secure, and safe environment. Crew problems are one of the main reasons owners sell their yachts. One of the toughest things for yacht owners and guests is never knowing what to expect when they come to the boat. They value longevity and count on you to keep service standards consistently high.

- **Lawful Behavior:** Observe and obey all local, national, and international laws; do not engage in illegal, immoral, or unethical behavior. Regardless of what you think is acceptable behavior, there are legal and regulatory concerns for lawful activities at sea. For example, if you or a crewmember or a guest are caught with illegal drugs, the captain and any licensed officers are at risk of losing their credentials. You will most certainly lose your job, but they could lose their careers. Not to mention, the yacht could be seized.

- **Commitment:** Be a professional. This career is not for the faint of heart, and it will require a lot of personal sacrifice. The rewards are well worth it!

    o   Do your best to meet and exceed service expectations and

standards;
- Challenge yourself to expand and improve your abilities;
- Make every effort to be consistent in your actions;
- Take responsibility for the tools and materials you work with;
- Be an example to others by elevating the art of service;
- Maintain appropriate professional boundaries in your relationships;
- Promote a healthy sense of respect and commit to the highest level of care for all persons and property associated with your employer;

- **Conduct:** Uphold high standards concerning your personal behavior, your professional image, and your overall character. Avoid engaging in any activities that could damage your reputation as a professional yacht stew. Think twice about any photos you post on social media—your friends and family are not the only ones who will be looking at them. You will be judged accordingly.

- **Personal Development:** Develop a high level of self-awareness and objectivity; overcome judgmental attitudes and work at personal and professional development.

- **Leadership:** Keep a positive attitude and perspective as a professional. Encourage finding positive, constructive solutions to problems. Even if you are not in a management position, lead by example. If you are well-qualified for your position, help your supervisor out by managing up. Be a help, not a hindrance.

- **Professional Relationships:** Work to maintain appropriate relationships and boundaries in every aspect, including religion, family politics, sexuality, and the use of your owner's property. Have the courage of your conviction.

Confidentiality and Gossip Control

"Great minds discuss ideas. Average minds discuss events. Small minds discuss people." —Eleanor Roosevelt

Almost everyone is familiar with the adage "loose lips sink ships." While the phrase comes from World Word II espionage, today this phrase is true for an entirely different class of ships, namely yachts. Anyone familiar with the lives of the wealthy and famous understands that their lives are constantly under the scrutiny of the paparazzi. It is unfortunate that some members of the press don't respect the traditional boundaries enjoyed by the rest of us, i.e., our private lives are off-limits to prying cameras and reporters. Yachting offers one of the few opportunities left for the wealthy and famous to enjoy part of their lives in the privacy the rest of us take for granted. As a member of a yacht's "inner circle," it is critical that you always honor the confidential nature of your employment by never disclosing any knowledge that you may gain about your employer(s) or the guests on board the yacht.

In a similar manner, to ensure that good discipline is always maintained aboard the yacht, you must take an active role not only by not spreading gossip but also by taking steps to curtail any rumors that may be going around. Inappropriate use of social media has become a problem for many yachts, when crew members post confidential information on personal pages.

Personal Hygiene and Grooming

It may surprise you to learn that there are strict regulations regarding appearance on the job. Your professional image reflects upon your consideration of yourself, other crew, the captain, the owner, and the yacht itself. Your appearance tells a lot about your personality and attitude. As a yacht steward or stewardess, you are on display at all times and captains, owners, guests, crew agents, and other crew will be judging you, and what they see reflected in your appearance and attitude. Rules and regulations for proper uniform and dress code will often be included in your employment contract or agreement.

You will be expected to implement proper grooming habits at all times. You are always on view. Your personal grooming includes not just your uniform and your smile, but also your hair, hands, teeth, posture, and figure. As for personal hygiene, shower daily and brush your teeth frequently. Avoid eating foods that will cause bad breath when you have to be in close contact with guests. For stewardesses, keep your hair clean and neat and under control; long hair should be kept tied back away from your face. Do not wear a lot of makeup. Excessive piercings are not acceptable; limit jewelry to simple, classic earrings. Your nails should be clipped short and conservatively polished—no extreme nail art. Only natural or very pale polish is allowed at all. Go easy on cologne or avoid it entirely. Visible tattoos are unacceptable.

Apply the rules of proper safety, sanitation and hygiene for food service operations. Keep your hands away from your face, hair and eyes, and wash them frequently. Keep your fingers off the plates when you are handling or serving them; hold them by the edges only. Pick up glasses by the base, not the rim. Use only clean white towels in service, and never use them to wipe your face or hands. As tempting as it may be to steal a taste of the wonderful meals that your celebrity chef creates, do not pick at food or taste it with your fingers; use a clean fork or spoon.

Demonstrate grace and self-confidence at all times. Know the rules of proper speech, grammar and diction. Be conscious of your speech and choose your words carefully; never use slang or swear words. Think twice about what you say in the presence of guests. Do not say or do anything to compromise their opinion of your professionalism.

Be conscious of the proper dress code and uniform at all times. Make sure your uniform is clean and tidy, and always have a back-up ready. Wear appropriate attire in any situation where you will be interacting with guests, such as going swimming or to the beach, or when invited to join them for dinner ashore. Take care that your attitude, personal dress code and the image you project is a reflection of your professionalism. You might discover that your owners are more impressed with modesty than in the amount of skin exposed when crew are invited to accompany them on outings. Dressing to dine with your owners is not the same as dressing to go out with crew.

Privacy Rules and Professional Boundaries

"Understanding the connection between boundaries, accountability, acceptance and compassion has made me a kinder person." —Brene Brown

In order to build solid working relationships, you need to develop rapport and trust with everyone onboard. As the yacht's central figure for service, it is your job to make sure that everyone feels at ease approaching you, relating to you, asking you questions, and considering your suggestions or advice. Successful working relationships are anchored by a clear understanding of what your role is and, perhaps even more importantly, what your role *isn't*.

The following principles serve as a guide to maintaining privacy rules and professional boundaries:

- Refer to the owners with a formal surname at all times. If they insist otherwise, you should suggest finding a compromise such as Mr. and Mrs. X.

- Be mindful when socializing with owners, guests and other staff. You must maintain the ability to manage this environment. If alcohol is being consumed, inhibitions will be lowered and you must remain in control of professional boundaries and proper safety procedures at all times.

- Do not use the position of your owners or guests for personal gain or to request personal resources such as tickets for sporting events or performances. Occasionally, these may be offered as bonuses; only then is it appropriate.

- During entertainment events, maintain professional boundaries. Keep conversations with guests short and polite. Safety and security come first.

- Set a "no gossip" policy and help your co-workers uphold it.

- Watch for unhealthy relationship changes and avoid co-dependent behavior. Keep your personal life private within reason.

- o *This is really important*: When an owner or guest chooses to be friendly with you, it can be hard to maintain appropriate boundaries, but this is crucial. No matter how "close" you have become, you are not part of the family. Never, ever go above your department head or the captain's level of authority because you think you have a "special" relationship with owners or guests. Your bags will be on the dock in no time, and you will have a one-way ticket home.

- It is not appropriate to share your opinions, and it can be awkward if you are asked to do so. If asked for an opinion, state that your business is the care and well-being of the family. By the same token, give advice carefully if it is requested of you. Do not put yourself, your safety, your professional reputation, or your job in jeopardy with careless banter with the guests.

- Do not make judgments about disputes or events within the family. You will be in a position to overhear many private conversations. Do not allow yourself to be drawn into quarrels if you are present in the room, and do not take sides. Leave the room if possible. If physical violence takes place, notify the captain at once.

In Summary:

In accordance with the guidelines established by the Professional Yachting Association stews are expected to know the following about guest services/etiquette:

- Demonstrate the proper way to greet and to say goodbye to guests/owners. Know how to properly execute a handshake; how to make introductions; the importance of using a clear and polite tone of voice; how to make the correct eye contact; proper dining etiquette when invited to dine with guests and owners

- Proper forms of address, diplomatic protocol, proper demeanor and courtesy for international guests and crew

- How to present a warm, professional, gracious demeanor around guests

- Understand and demonstrate the importance of punctuality
- Understand the importance of personal and professional boundaries with guests and crew
- Understand proper manners and know how to behave around guests while working and during service
- Have an understanding of cultural differences between nationalities and of the conduct adjustments that may be needed for owners, guests, and crew
- Understand and respect the religious and dietary preferences of different nationalities for both guests and crew
- Be aware of the importance of proper hygiene and health issues. Complete medical check-ups and practice dental hygiene; obtain any vaccinations needed for travel; hygienic behavior and personal habits
- Know and demonstrates the importance of personal cleanliness, hygiene, and organization in cabin and all crew areas
- Understand requirements of proper uniform and personal presentation
- Understand the concept of professional appearance and how to stand and present oneself on deck when coming into and leaving port
- Understand and respect the aspect of uniform and what it represents to the individual, fellow crew members, owner, captain, and reputation of the yacht
- Know and demonstrate the use of duty rosters and scheduling for housekeeping matters. cleaning and service
- Comply with watch schedules and standing orders for bridge assistance underway

Chapter 3

Training Requirements

Technically speaking, you can start working as a junior or 2nd stew without having any formal training at all, but don't expect that to last for long because ship Captains are required to have trained crew members for safety reasons. The mandatory safety training is covered in the Standards of Training, Certification & Watchkeeping (STCW) '95 As Amended basic safety training.

Standards of Training, Certification & Watchkeeping (STCW) '95 As Amended

The International Maritime Organization (IMO) comprises 133 signatory countries from around the world. As an agency of the United Nations, the IMO is responsible for the safety and security of shipping as well as the prevention of marine pollution by ships. In 1995, the IMO, acknowledging that over 80% of transportation accidents are caused by human error, created the requirement that all professional mariners with designated safety or pollution prevention duties on a vessel's muster list must have a Basic Safety Training course and a basic security course and receive STCW Compliant Certification. You must have this certification.

The cost of STCW varies by school in accordance with the teaching methods used (e.g., pool vs. at sea,) but it is generally around $900 in the United States. The course is divided into four modules, which may be taken and paid for at different times, thereby making it more affordable. European schools typically charge more, so expect to spend 1,200-1,500 Euros.

Locating the schools nearest to you is easy; simply Google "STCW training," and perhaps the largest city you are near to, in order to obtain a listing. Maritime Professional Training in Fort Lauderdale offers this course every week, and other schools offer it regularly as well.

The complete STCW training is a five-day course and may be taken by anyone who is over 16 years of age and in reasonable health. The four modules of the STCW '95 training are:

- Personal Water Survival;
- Fire Prevention & Fire Fighting;
- Personal Safety & Social Responsibilities;
- Elementary First Aid & CPR.

Personal Water Survival

The Personal Water Survival training is typically 1½-2 days in length. You will probably spend a day in a classroom learning subjects such as the types of emergency situations (e.g., collision, fire, floundering), the types of life-saving gear and electronics normally carried on yachts, the location of personal life-saving gear, and the principles concerning survival at sea. You will then be instructed and required to demonstrate your skills in how to don a life vest, how to don and use an immersion suit, how to safely jump from a height into water, how to right an inverted life raft while wearing a life vest or immersion suit, how to swim wearing a life vest or immersion suit, how to keep afloat without a life vest, how to board a survival craft from a ship and from water while wearing a life vest or immersion suit, what initial actions to take after boarding a survival craft, how to stream a drogue or sea anchor, how to operate survival craft equipment, and how to operate location devices including radios.

Fire Prevention & Fire Fighting

The Fire Prevention & Fire Fighting portion of STCW is usually two full days in length. The training is intended to make sure that you know how yacht fires are caused and the precautions that should be taken to minimize the risk of fire on ships. It teaches you to maintain a state of readiness, to respond to emergency situations involving fires aboard ship, and to perform as a member of a fire-fighting party, including the use of a self-contained breathing apparatus. The course is designed to lead to competency in the location of fire-fighting equipment and emergency escape routes, the fire triangle, the types and sources of ignition, flammable material controls, fire and smoke detection, alarm systems, and the classifications of fire and approved extinguishing agents.

Personal Safety & Social Responsibilities

The duration of the Personal Safety & Social Responsibilities portion of STCW training is typically a half-day in length. The purpose is to provide you with a basic introduction to safety procedures and accident prevention. The training will also familiarize you with the employment and working conditions on board merchant sea vessels or private yachts, and you will learn how to conduct yourself professionally at all times. The course teaches you how to take proper measures to prevent pollution of the marine environment, how to observe safe working practices, and how to understand orders and be understood in fulfilling your duties. You will also learn how to be a positive force contributing to effective human relationships among the crew and passengers. Lastly, the course will teach you about health and hygiene issues at sea.

Elementary First Aid & CPR

This portion of training is typically 1-1½ days in length. The objectives are to provide stew attendants with the knowledge and skills to be able to take immediate action upon encountering an accident or other medical emergency at sea. In this course, you will learn the precise steps to follow in various emergency situations. The training includes instruction in how to position an injured person and how to apply shock management techniques. You will learn to perform the latest cardiopulmonary resuscitation (CPR) techniques, how to use an Automatic External Defibrillator, and how to perform the Heimlich Maneuver. You will also learn: how to suppress bleeding, how to apply appropriate measures in the event of burns and scalds (including electrical and chemical burns), how to create a splint, and the basic human body structure and its functions.

STCW 2010: Manila Amendments

In 2010 a review of the STCW was conducted and the published results are known as the "Manila Amendments." These amendments are scheduled to be implemented by January 1, 2017. The purpose of the amendments is to ensure that the necessary worldwide standards will be in place to train and certify seafarers to operate the more technologically advanced ships in the future. The amendments create a major revision to the STCW '95 and will therefore significantly revise the training. Among the amendments adopted were a number of important changes to each chapter of the Convention and Code, including:

- Improved measures to prevent fraudulent practices associated with certificates of competency and to strengthen the monitoring and evaluation of compliance with the Convention.

- Revised requirements on hours of work and rest, as well as new requirements for the prevention of drug and alcohol abuse. There is also an update to the standards relating to the medical fitness of seafarers.

- New certification requirements for able seafarers. Security Awareness certificates are now required of all crew onboard.

- New requirements relating to training in modern technology such as electronic chart display and information systems (ECDIS).

- New requirements for marine environment awareness training and training in leadership and teamwork. Captains and heads of departments are required to complete leadership and teamwork courses and it is recommended for chief stews as well.

Guidelines for Unified Excellence Service Training (GUEST)

One of the challenges of yachting has always been the lack of an aptitude or competency standard for interior staff. Deck and engineering departments have strict standards, because licensing requirements are governed by regulatory bodies; interior service is not. This means that, on the one hand, interior crew may not know what is expected of them from one boat to the next, and on the other hand, owners may not know what skill sets they are getting from one stew candidate to the next. Training is vital.

The Professional Yachting Association (PYA) has accepted the task of developing a formal training and certification requirement standard for interior yacht crew, and progress is moving along nicely towards international recognition. The objective is to put into practice a formal training and certification requirement standard that will recognize and issue certification for specific levels of experience, training and knowledge. There is a competency exam system in place now for qualified and properly trained crew to get credit for their experience, allowing stews to apply to test out of the system without being required to repeat classes.

This is exciting news. There has been very little formal training available, and up until now there have been varying standards and objectives for what little training exists. The lack of interior standards is absurd, because interior staff are on the front line with owners and guests and have the greatest amount of contact.

Why Training? Why Now?

"What gets measured gets managed." —Peter Drucker

Ever since I began my yachting career I have felt that Interior Crew are at a disadvantage because we have little empirical data to measure in order to determine learning and progress. Much of a stew's service capacity is based on soft skills that are a reflection of personal values, such as habits, attitudes, communication facility, and social graces.

As difficult as it is to measure proficiency in this area, we have to build a framework for a basic system of measuring and managing the progress of these skills. One common solution is to use checklists and task sheets, along with frequent inspections and regular feedback on the sequence of service delivery, to make sure that expectations are being met at every step.

The fact remains that a large part of our job is based on subjective experience. Take meal service, for example. Etiquette theories aside, there is no single, universally accepted definition of a "right" or "wrong" way to serve meals on every yacht. Whatever the owner, charter guest, or captain dictates as policy determines what type of service we deliver. We may know the "correct" rule, (after all, we just took a Silver Service course), but in reality, the right way for a particular boat is based on subjective interpretation. Basically, whatever the owner or chief stew says is "the rule" determines what type of service we deliver.

Proposed New Professional Training Requirements

The Professional Yachting Association (PYA) proposed a new formalized structure for the training and certification of interior crew working on large yachts, called the Guidelines for Unified Excellence Service Training (GUEST). It was developed in close consultation with all industry stakeholders including interior crew, captains, training providers, charter agents, and crew agencies. Training providers will be able to apply for certification to show that their training meets the PYA GUEST criteria, thus ensuring that students of their classes are receiving the proper and appropriate training.

It is not mandatory certification for stews or for training providers, but it provides a guideline of which courses individual training providers and schools should offer, and also gives interior crew a way to record their level of competency, service skills and the time they have spent at sea. It positions them at a higher level for employment, and also helps captains make decisions in the hiring process, by presenting them with legitimate standards.

The effects of this new training standardization should not be underestimated. Yacht owners will finally have an objective standard for measuring the performance of stews. They will come to expect, and require, these standards from all stew crew members. Equally important, stews will have a baseline for measuring their own performance, and for determining additional training needs. The sooner stews obtain this level of training, the better positioned they will be for future employment in the industry. It will also give them a record of training and skills that they can take with them and use in other fields outside of yachting.

PYA Interior Crew Training and Certification Development route

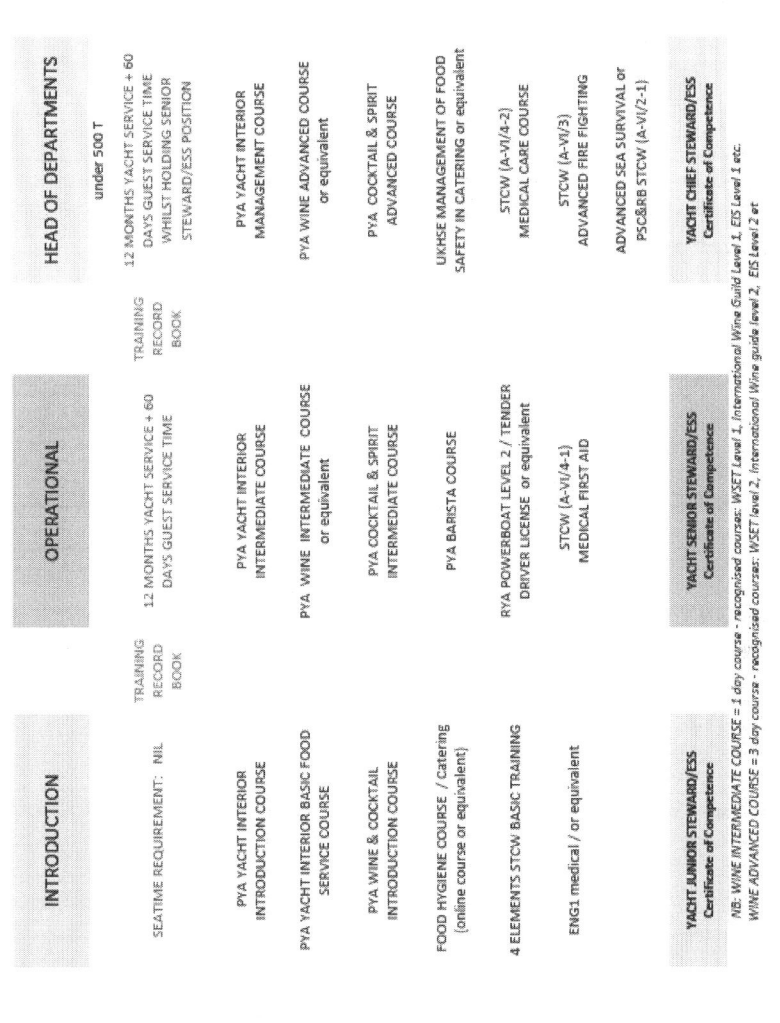

INTRODUCTION

- SEATIME REQUIREMENT: NIL
- PYA YACHT INTERIOR INTRODUCTION COURSE
- PYA YACHT INTERIOR BASIC FOOD SERVICE COURSE
- PYA WINE & COCKTAIL INTRODUCTION COURSE
- FOOD HYGIENE COURSE / Catering (online course or equivalent)
- 4 ELEMENTS STCW BASIC TRAINING
- ENG1 medical / or equivalent

YACHT JUNIOR STEWARD/ESS
Certificate of Competence

OPERATIONAL

TRAINING RECORD BOOK

- 12 MONTHS YACHT SERVICE + 60 DAYS GUEST SERVICE TIME
- PYA YACHT INTERIOR INTERMEDIATE COURSE
- PYA WINE INTERMEDIATE COURSE or equivalent
- PYA COCKTAIL & SPIRIT INTERMEDIATE COURSE
- PYA BARISTA COURSE
- RYA POWERBOAT LEVEL 2 / TENDER DRIVER LICENSE or equivalent
- STCW (A-VI/4-1) MEDICAL FIRST AID

YACHT SENIOR STEWARD/ESS
Certificate of Competence

HEAD OF DEPARTMENTS

under 500 T

TRAINING RECORD BOOK

- 12 MONTHS YACHT SERVICE + 60 DAYS GUEST SERVICE TIME WHILST HOLDING SENIOR STEWARD/ESS POSITION
- PYA YACHT INTERIOR MANAGEMENT COURSE
- PYA WINE ADVANCED COURSE or equivalent
- PYA COCKTAIL & SPIRIT ADVANCED COURSE
- UKHSE MANAGEMENT OF FOOD SAFETY IN CATERING or equivalent
- STCW (A-VI/4-2) MEDICAL CARE COURSE
- STCW (A-VI/3) ADVANCED FIRE FIGHTING
- ADVANCED SEA SURVIVAL or PSC&RB STCW (A-VI/2-1)

YACHT CHIEF STEWARD/ESS
Certificate of Competence

HEAD OF DEPARTMENTS

above 500 T

Half the required Management entry level Yacht Service & Guest Service will be on vessels over 500gt for those applying for above 500gt Management level

- STCW MANAGEMENT COURSE
- 5 DAY YACHT ACCOUNTING & BUDGET COURSE
- INTRODUCTION TO INTERNATIONAL SAFETY MANAGEMENT'S COURSE or equivalent

PYA WRITTEN AND ORAL EXAM

YACHT CHIEF STEWARD/ESS
Certificate of Competence

NB: WINE INTERMEDIATE COURSE = 1 day course - recognised courses: WSET Level 1, International Wine Guild Level 1, EIS Level 1 etc.
WINE ADVANCED COURSE = 3 day course - recognised courses: WSET level 2, International Wine guide level 2, EIS Level 2 et

Rev 22

[Image courtesy of www.pya.org]

PYA Standard Interior Requirements

Level 1: Introductory Interior Requirements

The yachting industry is unique in the hospitality field, and stews should have a good basic understanding of how things work. An interior introduction course should be taught as a full time course of at least 24 hours delivered over three days. The PYA standard requires stews to understand the demographics of the yachting industry and how to professionally search for a position. Also, information about Interior Crew employment matters including salary, contracts, resumes, and agents is required to be a part of a class like this.

Students are expected to be familiar with the main departments of a yacht and the chain of command within each one. They are expected to understand and demonstrate the presentation and detailing of cabins, bathrooms, and other guest areas; know how to clean and maintain the fabrics, surfaces, and finishes found on a luxury yacht; and also comprehend laundry procedures. In addition, they are required to understand the health and safety issues within the interior areas of a yacht.

A course like this should also introduce guidelines on international protocol, and education on the importance of communication and skills regarding the etiquette of meeting and interacting with guests from different cultures and regions of the world. It should emphasize the cultural differences among American, British, Asian, Russian, European, and Middle Eastern guests and cover the correct use of various forms of address including titles.

PYA Standard Basic Food Service Certificate Requirement

A large part of a stew's job revolves around food and beverage services. There are certain things that stews are expected to know. A Basic Food Service course certificate that meets PYA standard requirements is intended to make sure stews know how to provide food and beverage services properly and hygienically aboard a yacht. They should understand all aspects of private and charter yachting, including the demographics of the industry, the accepted definitions of "service," and the role of the interior crew in providing service. This includes an understanding of menus and culinary terms as well as how to set up for service in all areas on a yacht.

Server training begins with knowledge of correct table settings, and the proper, sanitary way to handle flatware, glasses, and china during setup and as the meal is served. Stews will learn about their own personal presentation skills, including: attention to detail, self-assurance, poise and bearing, the importance of personal hygiene, correct dress, and promptness.

Stews are expected to understand the different food and beverage table service styles employed for breakfast, lunch and dinner service including: Silver Service (French, English and Russian), and Plated Service (American). They should also learn about providing a variety of food services including: caviar, hors d'oeuvres, canapés and appetizers, BBQ, room service, and buffet. A course should also incorporate table setting and decorations and the basics of beverage (tea, coffee, cocktail, wine, water) services.

PYA Standard International Food Service Requirement

A yacht crew is often comprised of people of different nationalities working together as a team. Each one of them may have different definitions and understandings of the various styles of food, beverage, housekeeping, and personal service that are provided on yachts. This can create misunderstandings and confusion. One of the goals of an International Food Service training course that meets the requirements of the PYA criterion is to eliminate language barriers aboard yachts by standardizing a glossary of global common menu terms, service procedures, and dining classifications. This comprehensive glossary of common international menu terms is available for download on the pya.org website.

For example, "hors d'oeuvres" are also known as "appetizers" or "canapé," depending on the location. In Europe and South America, a starter is an entrée and means the first course. A "charger" may be known as a service plate, an under plate, or a liner plate and there are several different customs regarding charger plates. Other areas of controversy concern whether to serve and clear plates from the right or the left, and whether it is better to eat food in the European or Continental style, or in the American or Zig-Zag style. These are the two dominant styles of eating utensil etiquette employed on private yachts:

The European style, also referred to as the **continental style**, is to hold the fork in the left hand and the knife in the right throughout the meal. Once a bite-sized piece of food has been cut, it is directed straight to the mouth by the left hand. The fork tines always remain pointing down. The knife and fork are both held with the handle running along the palm and extending out to be held by thumb and forefinger. This style is sometimes called "hidden handle" because the palm conceals the handle

Continental Style

Cutting food - American & Continental style

Eating Continental style

Continental style - I'm resting position

Continental style - I'm finished position

The American style, also referred to as the zigzag method, the knife is initially held in the right hand and the fork in the left, just as in Continental dining. Holding food to the plate with the fork tines-down, a single bite-sized piece is cut with the knife. The knife is then set down on the plate, the fork is transitioned from the left hand to the right hand, the left hand is placed to rest in the person's lap, and then food is brought to the mouth for consumption. The fork is then transferred back to the left hand and the knife is picked up with the handle along the palm and the index finger pressing down at the neck of the handle.

American Style

American style - I'm resting position   *American style - I'm finished position*

[Images courtesy of professionalimagedress.com]

      Another service difference is that American-made flatware settings do not usually include a starter, salad, or luncheon knife. Because of this, many yachts order their silverware from European manufacturers in order to have all of the dining and service pieces on hand. Internationally, yachts will customarily be set up for continental style if the silverware service is complete.

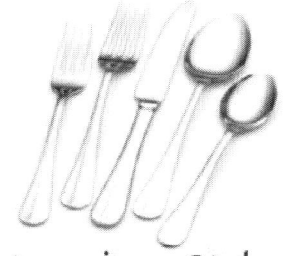

American Style   Continental Style

[Images courtesy of www.overstock.com and www.bettridge.com]

45

Level 2 PYA Standard Interior Requirements

Intermediate Requirements

When stews have mastered the basics of yacht interior service, they can move up to the intermediate level. The PYA standard for an intermediate level course requires a full week-long training course of 40 hours spread over a period of five days. On completion of this standard, stews are expected to be able to understand and properly administer all departments within the interior of a yacht, including the operation and management of the interior information system computer(s). They will be expected to apply different service styles aboard a yacht and to be efficient in providing valet and housekeeping services. The standard at this level also includes how to store and serve cigars and how to handle fresh flowers and plants.

In the *introduction* portion of this criterion, stews should learn about the departments that comprise the interior and the guidelines for operating each department. This includes the ability to establish a vision, a mission, and goals for each department.

The next requirement of a course like this is *interior administration,* where stews learn about yacht inventories and how to maintain them, as well as how to create checklists to make their management tasks easier. They should learn how to maintain a service guideline book and also a laundry guideline book. They are to be trained in the development and maintenance of daily, weekly, monthly, and even annual rosters, and they are expected to learn about the yacht's on-board information management system(s) including: specifications, standards, schedules, records, and contacts.

In the *food and beverage service* portion of such a course, stews learn about and understand the different service styles including: tray services/silver service (English, Butler, French & Russian), and plated service (American). They will be expected to learn how to successfully provide breakfast, lunch & dinner, buffet and banqueting service, room service, BBQ service, hors d'oeuvres, table service, and caviar service. Students shall be taught how to create table settings and decoration, and to properly serve food and beverages.

The *housekeeping and valet services* portion of the course requirement should provide the detailed training necessary to understand and perform a wide range of services including: packing and unpacking guest suitcases, wardrobe management, shoe care, as well as cabin day and turn down service. Stews will also be expected to learn cleaning methods for the cabin and public areas of the yacht, as well as yacht interior surface (marble, ceramics, wood, art, silver, gold leaf, and brass) upkeep and interior fabrics (suede, leather, silk) maintenance. They should learn to care for a variety of fabrics including cotton, linen, wool, silk, and polyester.

The *human resources* portion of such a course would cover essential matters including: recruitment, training, employee relations, performance management, compensation, and compliance with human resource rules and regulations.

The last two sections of this course requirement cover *cigar service* and *flower/plant maintenance*.

Level 3 PYA Standard Interior Requirements

PYA Standard interior management requirement

Once stews have mastered the intermediate level training, they are qualified to advance to interior management. An Interior Management requisite that meets the PYA standard covers 40 hours of training over a five-day period. A course like this should provide an introduction to service management, which would require that stews learn to set and monitor the vision, mission, and goals of the Interior Crew of a yacht.

Such a course should also provide training on implementing and managing inventories, checklists, department procedures, a service guideline book, a housekeeping book, the laundry guidelines, and shift rosters. It should teach how to manage the interior information management computer(s), and the interior financial planning. The financial planning portion would encompass budgeting, wages, and petty cash. This course requirement would also provide additional training in the management of food and beverage services, housekeeping and valet services, human resource management services, event and destination services, cigar service management, and flower and plant management services.

Other Beneficial Training

If you have made it this far in your training, you may already be feeling overqualified. However, there are many other types of specialty training, as well as college courses, that can help to provide you with a well-rounded resume. For example, you could take courses in advanced medical training, advanced security training, powerboat and tender handling, bartending, floral arranging, massage, food and wine pairings, accounting, computer technology, and hospitality management, all of which directly relate to the skills needed for Interior Crew and Interior Crew Management positions.

PYA Standard Wine and Cocktail Requirements

Introductory Level 1: Wine and Cocktail Requirements

Yacht stews are expected to have a good grasp of wine and cocktail basics and service. An introductory level wine and cocktail course that meets the PYA standard requirement is recommended to be presented as a one-day course of at least eight hours, divided into three sections:

- Introduction to the world of wine;
- Wine regions and grapes of the world;
- Spirits and cocktail services.

The PYA standard for such a course is meant to ensure that stews have a basic understanding of the world of wine, including knowledge about the regions and grapes of the world that are important to the yachting industry. They should also know how to serve wine, have knowledge of spirits, and understand how to prepare cocktails.

Ideally, stews would perform comparative tasting of at least four wines in order to present different styles of wines produced around the world, to demonstrate wine-tasting techniques, and to understand basic wine-making. Stews should also conduct food and wine taste matching and should be able to discuss faulty wines.

The major regions and grapes important to the yachting industry include the wine country in France, Italy, and Spain, as well as America, Australia, New Zealand, and South Africa. Stews should understand the main differences between New World Wines and Old World Wines, and to learn about the Noble Grapes, including Chardonnay, Sauvignon Blanc, Cabernet, Pinot Noir, and Syrah. Lastly, stews should understand fortified and aromatized wines.

Stews are expected to understand the main spirit styles and what they are made from, including vodka, cognac, tequila, rum, gin, and whiskey; and they should learn how to blend traditional cocktails such as margaritas and a dry martini.

Level 2: Intermediate Wine and Cocktail Requirements

After the introductory level has been mastered, stews are eligible to move up to the intermediate level. The PYA education standard for an intermediate level course is intended to be delivered as one-day course of at least eight hours. Such a course should offer participants a basic understanding of distilled beverages: vodka, gin, rum, tequila, and whiskey. Stews should learn how to make basic classic drinks and variations of them. A course like this should also teach how to use cocktail tools such as a shaker, a bar-spoon, a jigger, and a strainer, and stews will be required to read a drink recipe and successfully create it.

A theory portion of the requirement should include a brief history of alcohol and a basic knowledge of spirits. Stews should understand the components of a great drink, as well as the techniques such as shaking, muddling, and straining. They should recognize several basic recipes of well-known drinks, made from vodka, gin, rum, tequila, and whiskey.

Level 3: Advanced Wine and Cocktail Requirements

Upon completion of the intermediate level, stews qualify for the advanced level training. An Advanced Level Cocktail and Spirit education that meets PYA criterion requires 24 hours of training spread over a three-day period.

Such a course requires that stews know how to make an assortment of basic drinks and their variations. Stews should know the fundamentals of creating mixed drinks, and should be trained in both speed and efficiency. A course like this should include the history of alcohol and provide an in-depth knowledge of distilled beverages. Stews should learn to handle multiple orders, develop menus, create their own drinks, and understand balance and speed. They will be expected to learn up to 50 basic recipes of well-known drinks.

PYA Standard Barista Requirements

Yacht stews will be providing coffee and beverage service to guests of many different nationalities, and they are expected to know how to prepare the beverage variations that clients are accustomed to. A Barista course that meets the PYA requirement ensures that stews understand the history and techniques of coffee making. They should understand all aspects of an espresso machine (operating instructions, the grinder and the "grind," the glassware, cleaning and care) and the steps (machine, water, beans, and pressure) involved in brewing a perfect espresso and achieving perfect froth (the milk pitcher, positioning, milk, technique, and temperature). It should also include the history of tea and proper tea service, and the history and service of chocolate beverages.

Chapter 4

Guest Services: Formal and Informal Dining

"We are what we repeatedly do. Excellence then, is not a single act but a habit." —Aristotle

When anyone on board a yacht is talking about "service," they immediately think of the stewards and stewardesses. If you want to make sure that thought always brings a smile to their face, you will have to master all the skills of the trade.

Providing 5-star service across a wide-range of interior service matters ranging from serving on fine china to serving after-dinner drinks is essential. Most yachts have their own rules about service, and there are various styles, techniques, and methods that are acceptable.

Yacht food service skills include:

- how to properly set up for breakfast, lunch, and dinner meal service.
- the correct sanitary handling of silverware, glassware, stemware, and dishware.
- ability to identify the most commonly used flatware and serving pieces
- the appropriate condiments to put on the table.
- know the correct procedure and order of service for items such as water and wine, bread and butter, sauces, condiments, and any other items.

The Culinary Institute of America publishes an excellent service book with guidelines for all of the above: Remarkable Service, a Guide to Winning and Keeping Customers for Servers, Managers, and Restaurant Owners.

The goal is to make meal service appear smooth, efficient, and effortless. In all cases, it is important to know what the preferred method of serving is on your yacht.

A Brief History of Formal Dining

In her book, *The Rituals of Dinner*, Margaret Visser leads us through the origins, evolutions, peculiarities, and classifications of table manners. According to Ms. Visser, formal dinners evolved from medieval and Renaissance models and were set up as a system by the 18th century. These formal dinner parties were not an everyday occurrence but were a ceremonial celebration of some sort, very expensive, and accessible only to royalty or heads of state.

There has always been a distinction between styles of service, most notably French Service as compared to traditional Russian Service. Keep in mind that the royal families throughout Europe were typically related by blood or by marriage, and in times of peace they would gather for ceremonies and special occasions. Information was spread and recipes shared and the traditions and methods of service styles began to blend together. It is logical that the French, the British, the Germans, and the Russians at one time may have all carved their meats at the table in the "French service" way, but they could call it whatever they liked, and in times when other countries were at war with France, they most likely did! The laws and rules of each country were made up by the ruling party and were subject to change at any time.

When restaurants came into being in Europe, three main styles of serving evolved based upon these main service styles. All food was prepared in the kitchen by the cooks, and then taken to the table on platters by the servers. Warm plates would be placed before the guests, and service would begin. In traditional Russian service, the meat would be pre-cut in the kitchen, then beautifully put back together on the platter so it could be presented to the diners as one piece and served along with the accompanying dish courses. In traditional French service, the meat was brought out on platters to show the guest and then it was carved, either in front of the diners, or taken back into the kitchen. The sauces and other foods were finished on a cart in a tableside display of artistry. In traditional British service, platters and tureens and covered dishes were placed on the table. The servers assisted diners in the beginning of the meal but then left the guests to help themselves.

Today, most restaurant food is pre-plated and portion controlled. In many countries, all pre-plated food is served from the right, while in America, the majority of restaurants train staff to serve from the left and clear from the right. As with so many aspects of service on a yacht, the proper way to perform food service is ultimately determined by the owner or the chief stew's wishes. It may be determined in part by where your guests are from geographically, and it may reflect traditions and norms of a particular group, country or religion. Food service on a yacht is also determined in part by the physical layout of dining areas, and accessibility to the table. Sometimes it is impossible to follow specific rules of service. In any case, the guests must feel confident in the staff's ability to make the correct service decisions that create a pleasant dining experience.

Silver Service

As a stew, you will be expected to know the fundamental serving style called "Silver Service" and its various methods. The styles used today are probably an adaptation of the French, Russian, and British service styles of the 1700-1800's. In the most general terms, it refers to the techniques of transferring food from silver platters assembled beforehand to the diners' plates. Silver serving utensils are used to perform this task; hence, the name "Silver Service."

In the classic service style used by most professional butlers, the service is performed using a fork and spoon in one hand. There is no single right or wrong way to perform food service at the table; what is correct varies from one yacht to the next, depending on whatever techniques meets the standards and expectations of the yacht's owners or guests. Many yachts have developed a more modern style of food service that combines various features from several methods.

There are several methods of serving food at the table, with technical differences that set them apart. The methods are:

- French/Butler Service
- Russian Service
- Gueridon Cart Service
- Family Service
- English Service

Types of Silver Service

French Service

In its original form, this service was reserved for very formal dining. In the original form of French Service, diners would come to a table that was covered with food, arranged symmetrically and beautifully decorated to give the impression of opulence and abundance. This gave the host the opportunity to display all of their expensive silver and porcelain. All throughout the meal, servers would continually change the courses and the diners would help themselves to as much or as little as they liked. The first course would be soups and lighter dishes and side dishes. The second course would be various spectacular roasts, whole fishes and fowl, cream sauces, salads and vegetables. The third course would be cheeses, sweets, pastries and fruit. Various theatrical presentations occurred throughout the courses of the meal.

It has come in and out of style over the years. In true French service today, food is cooked and plated from a gueridon or flambé cart in front of the guests. In yachting, it is characterized as the style of food service in which food is brought from the galley on silver platters that are presented by the servers at the left side of each individual guest. The guests then help themselves by using the serving pieces to lift food onto their plates. This is also known as Butler Service.

[Images courtesy of www.lvmh.com and mon-maitre-d-hotel.restautantemploi.com]

Russian Service

Russian monarchy favored this service and introduced it to France. In its original form, it was very elaborate, with many different platters and serving bowls used to create a dramatic effect. Great French chefs who had served at the court of Russian royalty popularized the "Russian" method of service in France in the 1800's. Dishes began to be served in succession, rather than presented all at once in an ornate table display. After the soup and various entrees were served, an impressive roast of whole fish or fowl was presented to the host and guests so that everyone could admire it in its entirety. It was then either carved by servers in the dining room or taken back to the kitchen where it was divided into portions and put on platters. The servers carried the platters around to the guests and they helped themselves to whatever they wanted. Course after course followed, all carried around and offered to the guests to help themselves. In this style, the host was no longer counting on the display of silver and porcelain to impress his guests, but on the number of courses and thus the number of servants he could provide. Careful attention was paid to the decoration and presentation of each course, and dessert was the most spectacular part of the meal. Service *a la russe* was introduced in Paris in 1810 and by the 1860's it had completely replaced service *a la francaise*.

For true traditional Russian service to be carried out on yachts, all food is arranged on a silver platter. The platters are brought to the table, held in one hand and served from the left side of the guest, by the server, using a serving spoon and fork.

The Professional Yachting Association has modified the definition of Russian service to mean Family Style Service. Russian owners and charter clients typically want food platters and bowls set on the table.

[Images courtesy of wikipedia.com and www.propos-de-chef.com]

Chapter 5

Guest Services: Wine and Spirits

"Wine is sunlight held together by water." —Galileo Gallilei

Let's face it: people are on a yacht to enjoy themselves. They are unwinding from the cares of everyday living. The yacht stew can help people relax by having a thorough understanding of wine and spirits. This section offers practical and professional tips to assist you in providing 5-star wine and cocktail service.

There are three broad categories of wines:
- Table wines
- Sparkling wines and Champagne
- Fortified wines, including aperitifs and dessert wines, and after-dinner drinks (liqueurs, cordials, and brandy)

Each of these classifications is highlighted in this section to provide the background you need to understand the basics of wine.

Table Wines

The majority of wines that are served are referred to as *table wines*. They are produced in wine-growing regions all over the world. There are two classifications of wine regions: "Old World," meaning the traditional growing regions of Europe, and "New World," which are the Americas, Australia, South Africa, and so on. Old World wines are usually named for the region where they are grown, while New World wines are usually named for the grape variety they are produced from. Table wines have an alcohol content of between 8% and 15%.

To understand the wines from a particular **Old World** region, one must know the grapes that grow there. Following is a list of some of the major growing regions of France, Spain, and Italy along with some of the most famous grape varietals grown in each region. For example:

- **France**
    - Burgundy-Chardonnay; Pinot Noir
    - Loire Valley-Sauvignon blanc
    - Champagne-Chardonnay; Pinot Noir
    - Beaujolais- Gamay
    - Alsace-Riesling,
    - Rhone- Syrah
    - Provence-Syrah
- **Spain:**
    - Rioja-Tempranillo
    - Ribera del Duero-Tempranillo
- **Italy:**
    - Tuscany-Sangiovese; Trebbiano
    - Piedmont-Barberra, Nebbiolo; Pinot Grigio

New World wines are named for the varietal of grape. New World growing regions include:

- North America
- South America
- Australia
- South Africa
- New Zealand

Noble Grapes

The study of wine is intricate and complex and can seem overwhelming. There are over 4,000 grape varieties, each having its own characteristic. However, of these 4000 varieties, there are only around 18 Grape Varietals that are considered Noble Grapes. Noble Grapes is a term used to describe the international variety of grapes that are the most recognizable for producing top quality wine.

To get started in yachting, we are expected to know the basics about several major white and red grapes.

Three Major White Grapes

The most important varieties among the major white grapes that you are expected to know about in yachting include: Chardonnay, Sauvignon Blanc, and Riesling. The growing regions and the production methods used create enormous variations in the style and flavor spectrum of wine produced.

Chardonnay is grown all over the world but its home is Burgundy, France. The aromas and tastes of Chardonnay range from apple and lemon through peach and melon with notes of nuts, butter, toast, and a creamy buttery aroma. Production methods vary distinctly by region and create great differences in style. France creates refreshing Chardonnay wines with notes of green apple, minerals, citrus, and grapefruit. It is used to make one of the great, classic, light wines, Chablis, which is legendary when paired with oysters. Following the general theory that wines of a region go best with that region's food, Chablis is grown on slopes that were once the shores of a tropical sea in the Jurassic era, and are full of ancient oyster shells. The limestone-rich soil gives Chablis the attributes that complement oysters so perfectly.

Sauvignon blanc is grown in France from the Gironde to the Loire Valley. Common types are Sancerre, Pouilly-Fumé, and Fumé blanc. The grape is also a component of the famous French dessert wines of Sauternes and Barsac. Today, Sauvignon blanc is becoming popular in New World wineries. It has distinctive vegetal and mineral descriptors. In California, Chile, and Australia, Sauvignon blanc tends to be dry, soft, and creamy. In South Africa, Sauvignon blanc is widely produced, with fresh squeezed grapefruit and lime added to the flavor spectrum.

Riesling produces some of the finest dry wines in the world and some seriously sweet wines. Most classic Riesling comes from Germany and Alsace, but Australia also produces some great varieties as well. Riesling can taste like fruits, honey, minerals, flowers, lime, and exotic fruits. Riesling has an enormous aging potential – up to 10 years or more. It is enjoying a bit of a revival because of its capacity to complement spicy foods, especially Thai and fusion cuisine. Riesling is very "terroir-expressive," meaning that it is influenced by the wine's place of origin. Late-harvest dessert wines and Eiswein are the most expensive wines made from Riesling.

3 Major White Grapes	
Chardonnay	• Notable regions: Burgundy, Champagne, So America, Australia, California
	• Wine aromatics: Apple, pear, vanilla fig, pineapple, melon, citrus, lemon, honey, butter
	• On the palate: Cool climate: zesty with med to high acid, medium body & alcohol. Warm climate: low to medium acidity, medium to high alcohol with a "round" or "fat" body.
Sauvignon Blanc	• Notable regions: Loire, Bordeaux, New Zealand, California, Italy, Chile, So. Africa and Canada.
	• Wine aromatics: Distinct vegetal aromas of cut grass, asparagus or green pepper, plus fruit notes of honeydew, grapefruit, gooseberry, green fig, and lemon or lime. Sometimes mineral scents
	• On the palate: High acidity, light to medium body, and medium alcohol.
Riesling	•Notable regions: Germany, Alsace, Italy, Austria, Australia, United States and Canada.
	• Wine aromatics: Young-lemon, lime, peach, minerals, beeswax and flowers. Older - gasoline, petrol. Dessert - apricot, honey, raisins, baked apple and peaches.
	• On the palate: High acid. Can be dry to fully sweet. Low to medium alcohol.

Four Major Red Grapes

The most important varieties among the major red grapes include: Cabernet Sauvignon, Merlot, Pinot Noir, and Syrah or Shiraz. As with white wines, the growing regions and the production methods used create enormous variations in the style and flavor spectrum of wine produced.

Cabernet Sauvignon is sometimes called the world's most famous grape, and is the king of the rich, dense reds. It is based in Bordeaux in France but it is grown just about everywhere in the world. It produces wines with high color, acidity, tannin, alcohol, and fruit, with a characteristically powerful blackcurrant aroma. The finest examples benefit from oak aging and have power and elegance. They are a key variety for the great wines of Bordeaux, including Pauillac and Margeaux. In Australia and New Zealand, Cabernet Sauvignon has a soft vanilla-laced aroma. Chile's Cabernet leans toward blackcurrants and plum, while California has enjoyed a huge success and its own style.

Merlot is grown in Bordeaux, France, which produces the serious wines with the serious price tags of the right bank of the Region's Gironde River, including St. Emilion and Pomerol. Merlot is also grown in the south of France for *vins de pays* (regional or country wines). It is also popular in Australia, South Africa, and New Zealand, as well as California. It is notable for its softer tannins and supple texture and is a popular choice in restaurants because it produces a soft, round wine that pairs well with many foods.

Pinot noir is one of the most difficult grapes to grow. It hails from Burgundy's Cote d'Or, in France, which is known for the famous wines of Pommard and Nuits-St-Georges. It is also grown in the Loire and Alsace and is one of the principal grapes in Champagne, where it is used as a blending wine. In Europe, it flourishes from Germany to Romania. California, Oregon, and New Zealand also grow Pinot Noir and do well with it. Pinot Noir tastes range from roses and raspberries, cherries and cranberries, to truffles and game. It is popular because it is less tannic than Cabernet Sauvignon and matures earlier, usually in 2-5 years. It produces elegant, silky wines.

Syrah or Shiraz is a dark skinned grape grown throughout the world and used primarily to produce powerful red wines. It is commonly known as Syrah throughout most of the world and is one of the major grapes of the Rhone Valley in France. In Australia, where it is the most planted red variety, it is known as Shiraz. California, South Africa, South America, New Zealand, Italy and Spain are also big producers. Syrah tastes like blackberry, with a whiff of smoke, chocolate, and violets. In Australia, it has chocolate, vanilla, and molasses scents. Overall, it has a spicy, robust flavor.

Champagne and Sparkling Wines

True Champagne is only produced in the Champagne region of France. Other fine sparkling wines from other regions of France are known as *cremant*. Most wine-producing countries produce sparkling wines, such as Prosecco from Italy and Cava from Spain. The production methods used outside of the Champagne region are very similar to those used in France. Sparkling wines contain between 8% and 12% alcohol plus carbon dioxide.

4 Major Red Grapes	
Cabernet Sauvignon	• Notable regions: Bordeaux (left bank), Napa CA, Washington, Coonawarra Australia, Italy, Spain, South Africa, and Chile.
	• Wine aromatics: Cassis (black current) blackberry, black cherry, mint/eucalyptus, green bell pepper. Oak aging can add smoke, toast, tobacco, and vanilla.
	• On the palate: High acid and juicy. Moderate tannins, bright red fruit character, silky texture.
Pinot Noir	• Notable regions: Burgundy, Champagne, Oregon, California, New Zealand, Chile.
	• Wine aromatics: Cherry, strawberry, plum, raspberry, gamey, leather, mushrooms, "barnyard funk"
	• On the palate: High acid and juicy. Moderate tannins, bright red fruit character, silky texture.
Merlot	• Notable regions: Bordeaux (left and right bank) Italy, California, Washington, Australia, South Africa, Chile.
	• Wine aromatics: Black fruit, plums, cherries, fig, brown spices (nutmeg & clove), chocolate, coffee, vegetal (if under ripe).
	• On the palate: Medium acidity and tannins, rich & supple mouth feel
Syrah or Shiraz	• Notable regions: Rhone, Australia (known as Shiraz), Paso Robles CA, Washington.
	• Wine aromatics: Raspberry, blueberry, blackberry, plum, black currant, violets, carnations, rosemary, tobacco, black pepper, smoke, leather, bacon, chocolate, eucalyptus)
	• On the palate: Brawny to soft. Moderate acidity with medium to high tannins. Full body.

There are three major types of Champagne:
- Non-vintage – a blend of two or more harvests
- Vintage – from a single vintage
- "Prestige" Cuvee – from a single vintage with longer aging requirements.

Not every year is a vintage year. Each Champagne house makes its own decision as to whether or not to declare a vintage year, based on the qualities of the grapes and the wine produced.

Champagne is known as "the drink of kings," a fitting title since it originally comes from the city of Reims, where 25 French kings were crowned—from Louis the VII in 1223 to Charles X in 1825.

The champagne/sparkling wine method is very interesting and complex. It requires that grapes must be harvested by variety and by individual plot and that grapes from different plots of land must be fermented separately. This process begins as dozens of lots of still, not sparkling, wines for the producer, which is then blended together to fit the "house style." The house style is bottled, a little extra sugar and yeast are added, and it is sealed with a cap, like a beer cap. The bottles are then laid down horizontally in the cellar, as they need to rest to allow the sugar and the yeast to work. This process causes a second fermentation to be formed inside the bottle, which causes a carbon dioxide byproduct to be trapped inside the bottle. This trapped carbon dioxide from the second fermentation is what makes the wine bubbly.

The second fermentation also produces yeast sediment, called lees, that falls to the bottom of the bottle. If the yeast lees are left inside the bottle, the yeast will eventually break down and create enzymes and amino acids, which work to enrich the texture of the wine. The winemaker allows the wine to take on the flavors and aromas of the yeast, which takes at least one year, and then the sediment must be removed. In the Champagne region of France the minimum period for aging is 18 months; some producers leave their premium wines to age like this for up to five years.

When it is time for the yeast sentiment to be removed, the bottles are agitated to drive the sediment into the neck of the bottle and then the bottle is inverted and passed through a freezing solution. This produces a plug in the neck of the bottle, which contains all of the yeast sediment. The bottle is turned upright and the cap is removed. The yeast capsule is expelled from the bottle and more wine is added immediately to replace the wine lost in the capsule. A dosage of a sugar solution may be added as well as the final adjustment of the dryness or sweetness of the wine. To finish, a traditional sparkling wine cork is inserted.

Serving Wine

"Wine is bottled poetry." —Robert L. Stevenson

Once you have chosen the perfect wine, proper service can significantly enhance its enjoyment.

Temperature and Humidity

Wine breathes in the bottle and can be affected by odors, temperature and by vibration, so it is important to store wine properly. One of the most important things to consider when storing and serving wine is temperature.

Different types of wine have different storage temperatures and different serving temperatures, according to type. There are various opinions as to what the proper temperature for storage is, but the range should be between 45°F/7°C and 60°F/ 15°C. Store wine bottles horizontally to keep the corks moist. The humidity level should be between 74% and 95%; anything over 95% encourages mold growth.

Red wine is served at a warmer temperature than white wine because it vaporizes and releases its volatile compounds at a higher temperature. Too much vaporization can affect the bouquet of the wine, so red wine is served at a temperature slightly lower than that of the average room, or about 65°F/18°C. The expression *room temperature* comes from the days before central heating and air conditioning, when most rooms were a little warmer than a cellar. Today, the average room temperature is typically 68-72°F/20-22°C, so most red wines should be served slightly cooler than room temperature.

Red wine that is taken out of storage about one hour before it is served should be at just the right temperature. If the bottle feels too warm, it can be chilled in a refrigerator for 30 minutes to an hour. If it is too cold, it can be warmed in a bucket of tepid water for about 10 minutes. If red wine is served too cold, the tannins of the wine will be strong and taste bitter. Proper red wine serving temperature recommendations vary. Full-bodied reds, such as a Cabernet Sauvignon, may be served at about 64°F; while a light-bodied red, such as a Pinot Noir, might be served at 54°F. A 4 to 6-ounce pour is appropriate for red wine. After a bottle of red wine is opened, it will keep for about 3 days as long as it is recorked and refrigerated.

White and rosé wines have fewer tannins than red wines. The bouquets are delicate and vaporize at a cooler temperature and so they are served chilled. In general, the sweeter the wine, the colder it is served. However, if chilled for too long, light-colored wines lose their bouquet and taste. White and rosé wines will chill to the proper temperature in an ice bucket filled half with ice and half with water in about 10 to 15 minutes. You can add a handful of salt to increase the chill rate. The recommended temperature range for serving white wine is 45-50°F. Serving white wine too warm can cause an unbalanced taste with an alcoholic edge; serving it too cold suppresses the aromas and innate flavors. After a bottle of white wine is opened, it will keep for about 2 days as long as it is recorked and refrigerated.

Opening a Bottle of Wine

- Remove the metal foil covering the cork, using the blade of a knife or a special foil cutter. Make sure that no jagged edges remain on the pouring surface because this can interrupt the flow of the wine and cause unsightly drips.

- Wipe the outside of the lip to remove any dust or mold.

- Gently insert the corkscrew into the center of the cork and use a slow turning motion to ease the cork from the bottle. Try not to insert the corkscrew all the way through the cork or small particles may fall into the wine. Also, try not to use too much pressure to avoid crumbling the cork.

- Begin dislodging the cork. Move the lever arm down toward the neck of the bottle. Set the first set of ridges at the bottom of the lever arm on the lip of the bottle. Push down on the lever so that the cork begins moving upward. If necessary, use the second set of ridges on the lever arm to continue dislodging the cork.

- Make sure you have a firm grip on the bottle, and that the lever arm is firmly in place, before you begin pulling up. Otherwise, the arm might slip.

- Remove the cork. Pull up the handle of the sommelier knife's handle firmly. The cork should easily lift from the bottle with a slight pop.

[Image courtesy of wikihow.com]

Troubleshooting

If the cork doesn't lift from the bottle, screw the corkscrew in deeper, lift the cork using the lever arm, and try pulling on the handle again. If the cork won't budge, you may not have screwed the corkscrew in far enough. Twist it until there is only one twist remaining before using the lever.

Sometimes the cork will leave a residue on the inside of the bottle, so you may have to gently wipe the inside of the rim before serving. Save the cork to reseal the bottle.

Serving Wine

To serve a bottle of wine, hold it in your hand with the label facing the guest so they can see the label. Wrap a napkin around the neck to insulate chill, and pour down the inside of the glass. Twist the bottle slightly with your wrist as you finish the pour to avoid drips.

[Image courtesy of choosingservice.com]

Glassware

Another important part of wine service is glassware. As stated earlier, wine glasses are made in assorted shapes to balance the flavor and bouquet and to bring out the best qualities of specific wines. They are held by the stem to keep the warmth of your hand from affecting the temperature of the wine, thus keeping the wine at the proper temperature longer.

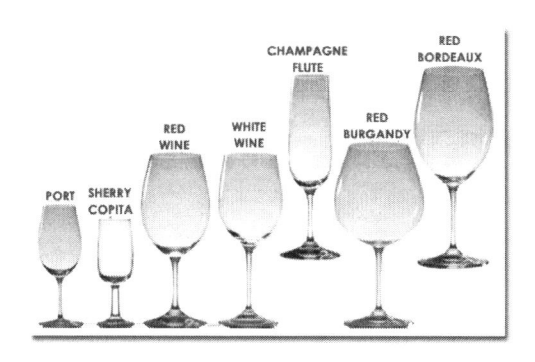

[Image courtesy of wineguidesuk.com]

Pour wine glasses to about half full to allow for swirling, which releases the characteristics of the wine, and for proper aeration. To develop the bouquet and aroma of red wine, it is served in a glass with a slightly larger bowl than a white wine glass, and the sides of the bowl curve slightly inward to enhance the flavor and bouquet.

Classifying & Evaluating Wine

The Color, Scent, and Taste of Wine

After wine is classified according to color and growing region, the complex and fascinating process of defining aroma, flavor and taste characteristics begins. Color, scent, and taste are important in learning to identify and classify flavors, sensations, and quality of wine. A great book that explains this process clearly and concisely is Kevin Zraly's *Windows on the World Complete Wine Course*. Keep in mind that discovering and enjoying wine is a very personal, subjective experience, and there is no such thing as a "right" or "wrong" perception. What any individual likes is what matters.

Color of Wine

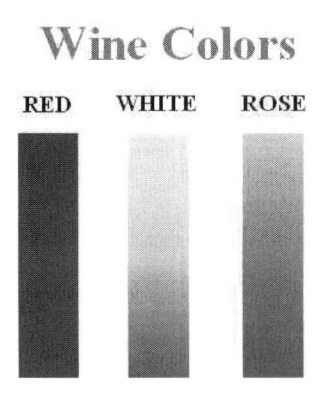

Wine Colors

RED   WHITE   ROSE

[Image courtesy of frenchwinetutor.com]

All grapes produce almost colorless juice. It is the pigment in the skins of the grape that gives wine its characteristic color. The color is determined by the length of time the skins remain in contact with the grapes/juice. As you gain experience tasting and experiencing wine, you will learn that color is usually a good indicator of the body of a wine, and can tell you a lot about the age of a wine and even where the grapes may have been grown. Swirling the wine in the glass and examining it is the first step in tasting and appreciating wine. It tells you about the color characteristics, the viscosity, and the body; it also aerates the wine in preparation for the next step in tasting.

White Wine: Not all white wine comes from white grapes. When red, purple, or black grapes are used, the skins, seeds and stems are removed immediately and the fruit is pressed to release the juice. Only the juice goes into containers for fermentation. White wine varies from soft yellow to deep gold. Young white wines range in color from pale yellow to yellow-green. The greenish tinge is from the chlorophyll present at the time of harvest. Mature white wines are usually a deeper shade, ranging from straw yellow to amber yellow to brownish yellow. The darker color is due to exposure to oxygen, just as cut fruit turns brown when exposed to air. Once a bottle of white wine is opened, it gains a little color.

Champagne is made primarily from white grapes, but occasionally black and purple grapes are used. Champagne will be pale yellow or rosé. Grown in a colder climate, the finest champagnes are pale to medium gold with a silver tinge and fine, steady bubbles. In champagne, the condition of the bubbles is a major visual clue about the wine.

Rosé wine is made from red or black grapes, most notably Syrah, Grenache, and Pinot noir. They are vinified using a special technique called *saignee*, in which the skins and solids remain on the grapes for a short time. Rosé wines range from soft purplish pink to an orange pink. The lightest rosé wines come from the Loire Valley in France, and also from California where they may be called Blush wines. Fuller rosé comes from southern France, Spain, Italy, and Australia.

Red wine is made from red, purple, or black grapes, with the skin and pips left on for an extended length of time. The longer the skins and pips remain on the grapes, the deeper the color of the wine and the more tannin there is in the taste of the wine. The level of tannin is an important component in the style of wine and its flavors and tastes. A high level can be astringent and bitter-tasting. Tannin is a natural preservative and helps the wine improve in the bottle. Red wine varies in color from bright, purplish red for young wines to deep scarlet, ruby, and mahogany hues for mature wines. The darker the color, the more tannins in the wine as it ages.

Judging the Appearance of Wine

For most wine lovers, appreciation and enjoyment of a wine's character begins with looking at the wine's appearance in the glass.

- **Clarity:** Wines may be described as cloudy, dull, clear, or brilliant. Hold the wine up to the light. Is it clear or cloudy? Red wines may have harmless particles suspended in the wine, while white wines may have crystals on the bottom which generally signify quality and richness of flavor.
- **Color:** The color can be seen by tilting the glass and holding it in front a white sheet of paper. Look through the wine where it meets the rim.
- **Depth of color:** Look straight down through the wine to see the depth of color.
- **Color clues:** The color of the wine can tell you about the climate of the vintage; the wine's age; they type of grape
    - White wines grow darker with age
    - Red wines are purple to ruby when new and fade to brick or dark amber colors as they age

The Bouquet and Aroma of Wine

Analyzing the scent is the second step in tasting and appreciating wine. With practice, you will learn to detect many aromas and scents that are the result of chemical components, such as esthers, ethers, and aldehydes, that are inherent in nature.

The scent, or nose, of wine consists of:

- Aroma – the scent of the grape varietals themselves.
- Bouquet – the complex collections of scents the wine exudes after fermentation and aging have taken place

The bouquet is released by gently swirling the wine in a glass. While all of our senses are involved in the enjoyment of wine, none is as powerful as *olfaction* – which is our sense of smell combined with our sense of taste. Both are related to the same area of the brain.

There are thousands of terms used to describe the scent of wine. More than 500 chemical compounds have been identified, and these are shared with fruits, vegetables and other more surprising substances (like chalk, leather, tobacco, and gasoline, to name a few). They occur naturally and regularly in wine; they are not added to the wine. There is no right way or wrong way to interpret the nose of a wine; your brain's interpretation of any aroma is all that counts.

To pair wine with foods, vintners use an official wine aroma wheel to describe wines in broad classes that identify the bouquet of the wine with nature. Some basic descriptions are:

- Fruity – indicates a bouquet and flavor similar to fruit, such as berries but not sweet.
- Earthy – faint taste of minerals, such as chalk.
- Grassy – has the aroma and taste of cut grass or herbs.
- Nutty – flavor similar to nuts, such as almonds.

It is helpful to know that, within each general classification of descriptors there are specific spectrums of flavors and aromas that are directly related to where the wine is from (e.g., cold climate vs. warm climate), production methods and aging processes, and the vintage of the wine (the weather and growing conditions of a particular year).

How to Judge Bouquet and Aroma of Wine

Swirling: Swirl the wine around inside the glass with a tight circular motion while holding the glass by the stem. Watch for the "legs" or "tears" as the surface tension of the wine breaks and the wine drips down the sides of the glass. As the surface tension of the wine breaks, the wine evaporates from the sides, and three components of the wine are released: the bouquet, the aroma, and the complexity of the wine.

Aroma: The aroma is the scent of the grape variety itself and will be affected by terroir and climate—the vineyard location itself, the weather, and the viniculture techniques that the producers use. It is used to describe the smell of freshly harvested grapes and is concentrated in the grape's skin and imparted into the wine during pressing and early fermentation stages. It diminishes over time and becomes a single element of the bouquet. Intensity of smell may be weak, light, medium, or full-bodied. Better wines have a more intense smell.

Bouquet: The bouquet of a wine is also know as a "nose." It is a complex collection of scents that develops during fermentation in the vat and as it ages in the barrel and bottle. The bouquet imitates the smell of fruits, flowers, spices, herbs, grass, nuts, and other more earthy smells.

Complexity: A well-developed bouquet is complex, layered, and consists of a variety of aromatics which can be difficult to identify. It is usually a very personal response and no two people will have the same response.

The Taste of Wine

It is hard to imagine having a vocabulary that is large enough to adequately describe the vast spectrum of wine flavors, tastes, and sensations. For white wines, it is helpful to begin by analyzing the taste of a wine in terms of various components, such as its balance of fruit/sugar, acidity, body, and alcohol. For reds, one needs to compare the balance of acidity, body, alcohol, fruit, and tannins. In both cases, the production and aging of the wine will create huge differences.

Tasting a wine confirms what our senses of sight and smell have told us about the wine so far; it is the next step in analyzing and appreciating the wine. Smell and taste are closely aligned. The nasal passages are connected to the centers of taste on the tongue and to the nerves in the brain located behind the nasal passages. Swirling the wine aerates it and releases the volatile compounds of the wine.

The next part of the tasting process is to aerate it more by gently and carefully "slurping" the wine. This sends the volatile compounds up from the back of your mouth to the olfactory nerve located at the top and back of your nose. From there the information travels to the limbic system of the brain, where it is interpreted by the individual.

The taste of wine is enhanced when wine is rolled around in the mouth several times, or "chewed," for about 15 seconds. (Longer than 15 seconds allows saliva to dilute the flavor and produce a watery taste.) This rolling action allows wine to coat all parts of the mouth and releases the four components of taste: sweet, acid, salt and bitter. It also gives you the first exposure to the sensations of the mouth-feel and body of the wine, which are important in helping you compare the balance of acidity and the bitterness of tannins. The locations of taste centers are:

- Sweet – tip of tongue; Examples of some terms associated with the sweetness of wine are very dry, dry, off dry, sweet, and very sweet.
- Acidity (a crisp, tart flavor) – sides of tongue; Examples of some terms associated with the acidity of wine are flat, flabby, lively, vibrant, crisp, and tart.
- Bitter – top sides of tongue, center of the back of the tongue; Examples of some terms associated with the bitterness of wine are tannic, soft tannins, medium tannins, firm tannins, bitter, harsh, and astringent.
- Salty – front and side of tongue. Salt is not tasted in wine.

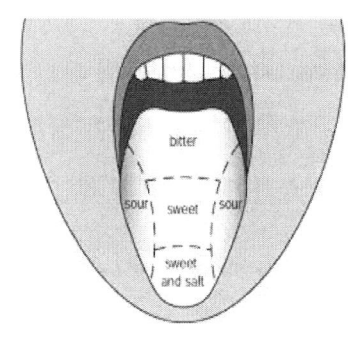

[Image courtesy of www.gigabiting.com]

Some examples of terms to describe the sensations associated with tasting wine are:

- **Sweetness:** Sweetness is experienced on the tip of the tongue. The later the grapes are harvested, the sweeter the grape. While the wine is fermenting, the sugar combines with yeast (both naturally occurring and those introduced in the wine making process) to produce alcohol. Sweetness is hard to judge because it is balanced by a wine's acidity and enhanced by the wine's fruitiness. Wines that are full of fruity flavors taste sweeter than they actually are.

- **Acidity:** Acidity is felt by the tastebuds on the sides of the tongue. They counter-balance sweetness and give a wine its liveliness and dryness.

- **Tannin:** Tannins produce the mouth-puckering quality found in red wines. Tannin comes from the grape skins, seeds and stems that are left in contact with the juice during fermentation and it also comes from the barrels used in aging. Tannins soften and diminish as a wine ages. Tannins produce the sensation of bitterness you taste at the rear center part of the tongue when you swallow red wine.

- **Body, Structure, and Mouth Feel:** Light, medium, full, rich are terms that are used to describe the weight or fullness on the palate as determined by the components of the wine.

- **Complexity:** How many different flavors and aromas can be detected

- **Balance:** Components of sweetness, acidity, tannin and alcohol should all be noticeable, but not overpowering. This is the most important part in the overall enjoyment in wine. In a balanced wine, no element is too weak or too strong.

- **Finish:** The flavors and sensations that linger in your mouth after you swallow the wine. Examples of terms may be short, long, delicate, intense, warm, bitter, or crisp, etc. Better wines have a longer "length" to their aftertaste and a more complex finish.

Beginning with grape varieties and vineyard locations, we have touched briefly on the very first basic steps in understanding and enjoying wine, namely the importance of the sight, smell, flavors and tastes of wine. The vintage year, which is the weather of a particular year, has a great deal to do with the quality of grapes that are produced in any given year. The vintner or producer is important as well, because it is their dedication and passion that influence the many decisions they make in their attempt to express the wine in the best way.

As we have seen, tasting wine involves all of the senses: sight, smell, touch, and taste – and let's not forget sound. When we ease the cork out of the bottle, or hear the soft sigh of a champagne cork being released, or clink our glasses together, we enhance the sense of anticipation. *Cheers!*

Spirits and Liqueurs

The study of spirits is every bit as interesting and complex as the study of wine and is peppered with stories of mystery, political oppression, and espionage. The alambic still was invented by Jabir Ibn Hayyan in the 9th century, probably as the result of experiments in alchemy; he is considered to be the grandfather of modern chemistry. Previous to that, the ancient Babylonians, the Egyptians, and the Chinese had learned to concentrate alcohol for use in perfumes and metal processing.

All spirits are made in the same way. A base ingredient containing sugar is fermented and the liquid is distilled to concentrate the alcohol. The raw materials of distillation are: water, starch, and fermentable sugars. These sugars come from: grains (cereal grains such as wheat, barley, corn and rye), used to make vodka, gin and whiskies; plants (potatoes, agave, sugar cane, and sugar beets), used to make vodka, tequila, and rum; and fruits (grapes, apples, plums, cherries, apricots, berries, and other soft tree fruits), used to make brandies, and various "eaux de vies." After distillation, the qualities of the spirit can be modified in a number of ways.

There are six main spirit classifications:

- Gin
- Whisky/Whiskey
- Vodka
- Tequila
- Rum
- Brandy

Gin

Gin is a grain distillate that originated in Holland and was originally called "genever," which was shortened to "gin." It is infused with juniper, along with a number of other botanicals, to give it its fresh, distinctive taste. Although gin is produced in countries all over the world, the British have historically dominated the gin market. Some of the classic big firms of the 18th and 19th century England include Booth, Beefeater, Tanqueray, Gordon's and Gilbey's.

[Image courtesy of www.thekitchn.com]

Gin has undergone a huge revival with the introduction of premium and ultra-premium gins and a renewed love of classic cocktails. A new style of gin was developed in 1988, based on Bombay gin. The pure spirit is vaporized and passed through at least 10 botanicals, rather than boiling the botanicals with the spirit before the second fermentation as had been done formerly. It is called Bombay Sapphire, and it ushered in a new era of gin production, favoring new brands in a "retro" British Empire style. Hendricks gin is made in Scotland and in addition to the traditional juniper infusion, it uses Bulgarian rose and cucumber to add flavor.

Gin is the base spirit for the classic Martini and the quintessentially British "gin and tonic."

Vodka

The word "vodka" is a Russian endearment meaning "little water" and it is distilled from various grains or plants such as potatoes. Polish and Russian vodka are the most famous brands and which of these countries can claim to be the originator of the drink is highly disputed between them.

Other European countries produce vodka, including Sweden, Finland Holland, and France, as does the United States. Some famous brands include Smirnoff, Stolichnoya, Absolut, Grey Goose, Ketel One, Belvedere, Finlandia and Ciroc. Cool climates are ideal for producing vodka. It is made from wheat, potato, corn, grapes, barley, or rye, and each has a specific body and style, texture, and flavor characteristics.

[Image courtesy of www.drinkinginamerica.com]

It is the base spirit in the Bloody Mary, the Screwdriver, and any number of vodka martini combinations.

Rum

The invention of rum came soon after the first sugar plantations were founded in the West Indies. In the early 16th century, sugar was a luxury product. The early explorers saw the potential of sugar production in the West Indian climate, both as an export product and, soon thereafter, as the raw material for another product: rum. Since yeasts feed on sugar for fermentation to produce alcohol, sugar was an obvious choice for distillation. Cane juice is boiled down to molasses, which then ferments and after distillation becomes rum.

[Image courtesy of www.manofthehourmag.com]

Today, rum is produced all over the West Indies and eastern South America, as well as in the Indian Ocean area, the USA, Australia, and Bermuda. There are many small, independent companies that grow sugar cane just for rum production. Bacardi, one of the biggest drink companies in the world, was founded in Cuba in 1862. During prohibition in America, Cuba became a hot tourist destination as the third generation of the Bacardi family invited Americans to come to Havana – and particularly to the famous Tropicana nightclub – to enjoy the music, dancing, rum and culture. The Bacardi company survived two revolutions in Cuba, first in the 1890's and again during Fidel Castro's regime. The Bacardi company and family finally left Cuba in the 1960's.

Other famous brands of rum include: Captain Morgan's (Puerto Rico), Mount Gay (Barbados), Meyer's (Jamaica), Goslings (Bermuda), and Pusser's (British Virgin Islands).

Rum mixes well with any number of fruit juices and goes well with cola. It is also the base spirit in the Daiquiri. Add a squeeze of lime to a rum and Coke and you have the famous *cuba libre*.

Whiskey or whisky

In cooler climates that could not produce grapes and thus could not produce wine, other raw materials were used to make alcoholic libations. Whiskey is made from a grain mash that produced a kind of beer, which was distilled to produce whisky, All whiskies are grain distillates. Today there are five major whisky/whiskey producing countries: Scotland, US, Ireland, Canada, and Japan. Its history is every bit as distinguished as that of cognac.

The Oxford English Dictionary reserves the spelling Whisky/Whiskies for those of Scottish, Canadian, or Japanese origin, whereas Whiskey/Whiskeys is reserved for those originating in Ireland or the United States. Both are still used today, and much is made of the distinction, but it's a well-known fact that you don't have to pass a spelling test to buy a wee taste of either.

Scotch whisky/whiskies: To be called true Scotch, this beverage must come from Scotland. There are over a hundred distilleries in Scotland, separated into six regions. Each region has its own distinctive style, influenced by the climate, the soil, the weather, and the proximity to the wild North Sea.

Scotch is a distillate from malted grains. After harvest, the grain is soaked in water to allow it to germinate. This is called malting. Next, the green malt is dried in kilns over peat fires, which give it its characteristic smoky flavor. The dried grain is ground, mixed with hot water, yeast is added and the fermentation process begins. It is distilled twice, and then aged in wooden casks.

There are 2 types of scotch: single malt, and blended or vatted malts. If it is a single-malt, it must be made from 100% malted barley grain from a single distillery. Examples of single malt are *Glenlivet, MacCallen's and Laphroag*. Examples of blended scotch are J&B, Johnnie Walker, and Ballantine's.

[Image courtesy of pernod-ricard..com]

Scotch is usually consumed straight up, on the rocks, or with water. It can also be used in a variety of whisky-based cocktails, but most connoisseurs prefer to savor it on its own.

<u>*Irish whiskey/whiskeys*</u>: The earliest recorded whiskey comes from Ireland, although the Scots would disagree. Irish whiskey is made in a similar manner to Scotch whisky, but Irish whiskeys have a notable mellowness from a mixture of malted and unmalted mash. It is triple-distilled in copper pots before aging, whereas Scotch whisky is mostly double-distilled. Irish whiskey is often described as mellow, sweet and fruity compared to other whiskies. At the beginning of the 19th century, Irish whisky was the most popular whisky in the world, and in the 1880's, after phyloxerra destroyed the cognac crop in France, it became the most popular spirit in the world.

A number of political developments have greatly undermined the Irish whiskey industry throughout history. In the 17th century there were over 100 distilleries; in 1988 there were 3, each producing a number of brands and styles. Today, increased demand for Irish whiskey has sparked new distilleries.

Common brands include Bushmills, Old Kilkenny, and Tullamore.

[Image courtesy of drinks.seriouseats.com]

<u>*American whiskey/whiskeys:*</u> Scottish, Irish and German settlers who came to America to escape famine in their own countries, and British rebels who came to escape persecution brought recipes and production techniques for their whiskeys with them. Recipes for malted barley and rye whiskeys were adapted to include the large amounts of corn grown in America. They were instrumental in the development of the spirit of the new nation. Two notable types are Bourbon whiskey and Tennessee whiskey.

> <u>Bourbon whiskey:</u> The first American whiskeys were made with rye and malted barley. Many distilleries were located in Maryland and Pennsylvania. Soon, however, Kentucky earned a reputation for its fertile soils and pure spring waters. Bourbon County, Kentucky, became well known in the late 18th century when distillers began producing pure corn whiskey. The county, and the whiskey, were named after the Bourbons, the French Royal Family, in recognition for their support of the American Revolution. The barrels used to transport the golden elixir to New Orleans were stamped in Mayville, Bourbon County, Kentucky, and legend has it that the name "bourbon whiskey" was born.
>
> Although it is most famously affiliated with Kentucky, whiskey may bear the "bourbon" label as long as producers follow a recipe and process that is set by law. Producers make bourbons in dozens of states. They have a distinctive taste from the barrels that the bourbon is aged in. They are new American oak barrels that are charred on the inside. This releases the flavors of the wood into the bourbon.
>
> There are two styles of bourbon: sweet mash and sour mash. Sweet mash is the result of normal fermentation, whereas sour mash, like sourdough,

uses a "starter" and is fermented twice. Examples of bourbon include Jim Beam, Wild Turkey, and Old Granddad. Maker's Mark and Old Forrester bourbons all use the Scottish spelling of the word, "Whisky" without the e. Old Forester has been continuously on the market longer than any other American brand. It was one of the only brands authorized for lawful production (for medicinal purposes) during Prohibition.

[Image courtesy of drinks.seriouseats.com and liquor.com and www.gooddrop.com.au]

Tennessee whiskey: Tennessee whiskey is essentially bourbon that is distilled and aged in Tennessee. Here the distillation process is taken one step further by filtering the whiskey through charcoal. This is called the Lincoln County Process. Sugar maple trees are burned, the ash is ground to a powder, and the whiskey drips through about three meters of finely ground sugar maple ash into mellowing vats before it is put into casks to mature. There are two main distilleries in Tennessee: Jack Daniels and George Dickel. Jack Daniels is one of the most beloved whiskeys in the world, and a Jack and Coke is probably the most popular drink to feature it.

Canadian whisky/whiskies: Canadian whiskies are a blend of rye, corn and malted barley. Rye is heavier-tasting and it is usually a small percentage of the final recipe. These blended whiskies have a reputation of being some of the lightest classic whiskies. Canadian law allows the addition of a small amount of sherry, port, or other fruit-based wines and the scent of the fruit is often present in these whiskies. Regulations for aging are different as well and many producers age their whiskey in barrels from Scotland, Porto, Juarez, or Bourbon.

Examples include: Hiram Walker, Seagram's 7, Canadian Club, Black Velvet, and Crown Royal. Crown Royal is a very popular whiskey with an interesting heritage. It is a blend of over 50 whiskies that was created to commemorate a grand tour of Canada by King George VI and Queen Elizabeth of England in 1939. It had the distinctive honor of being served aboard the Royal train.

[Images courtesy of liquor.com]

<u>*Japanese whisky/whiskies:*</u> Whisky production in Japan rose to prominence in the 1920's. Two men, Masataka Taketsuru and Shinjiro Torii are credited with founding the whisky industry in Japan. Masataka Taketsuru was a student of organic chemistry at Glasgow University in 1918. His family in Japan owned a sake distillery, so it seems logical that he would take employment in a whisky distillery. He married a Scottish girl, and they moved to the island of Hokkaido in Japan, which has a climate similar to Scotland's. He worked together with Shinjiro Torii, a pharmaceutical wholesaler who imported Western wines, port and liquor. They went on to found a whisky distillery that is now the Suntory distillery. Japanese whisky is modeled on single malts in the Scottish style, and is often aged in sherry or bourbon casks. Examples include Suntory, Nikka and Karuizawa.

[Image courtesy of boston-commonmagazine.com]

82

Mexican Tequila and Mezcal

Tequila is made from the plant with the botanical name, *Agave tequilana*. It is the national drink of Mexico, made from the chopped, pressed, and fermented hearts of the blue agave plant. To be called tequila, the finished product must be made from at least 51% to 100% blue agave juice. There are two different categories of tequila, and four different styles. The *mixto* category contains not less than 51% blue agave, the rest can be industrial spirit, or any other spirit made from a sugar distillate. The *pura* category contains any tequila that is 100% blue agave.

The agave plant looks like a cactus, but it is actually a member of the amaryllis plant, a type of lily. The heart of the agave is steamed or baked, and then cooled before being ground and pressed to release the syrupy agua miel, or agave honey. This sap is then mixed with water to form the base for distillation. It is distilled twice and aged in casks for a period ranging from a few months to several years.

Once tequila is classified according to the percentage of agave in the mix, it is also broken down into style designations, according to how long it is aged. White, or *blanco,* must be aged for a minimum of 60 days; gold, or *oro* is made much the same as white tequila, but with flavoring and color added, often caramel. *Reposado*, or rested tequila must be aged in oak for 60 days to one year; *Anejo*, or aged tequila must be aged for over a year.

[Image courtesy of eltequilarestaurant.com]

Mezcal, another product of the agave family, can be made from one of dozens of agave plants. The adage goes, "All tequila is mezcal, but not all mezcal is tequila." However, the Mezcal producers set high standards within the industry, with some brands being a minimum of 80% blue agave. The heart of the agave is roasted, not baked or steamed, which gives it a smoky flavor. It is a regional product, made in the state of Oaxaca. One of the most famous brands is Monte Alban, with the distinctive worm in the bottle. What's with the worm? Some say it adds character and sweetness. It is actually either a weevil larva, or a certain species of maguey worm. It seems more palatable once you know that certain worms are a seasonal specialty food in some parts of Mexico. Some people see the worm as a novelty item, some as an aphrodisiac, but there is no mistaking it as identifying a quality product with a character all its own.

[Image courtesy of drinkhacker.com]

Tequila and Mezcal are frequently served straight up in a small shot glass, accompanied by salt and lime. Favorite cocktails featuring tequila are the Margarita and the Tequila Sunrise. The popularity of tequila has skyrocketed since the 1990's, and producers are having a hard time meeting the demand quickly; the agave plant takes up to 10 years to mature.

Brandy

The term "brandy" generally denotes any grape-based spirit distilled from wine. It is the first know distillate. The name comes from the Dutch word, *brandewijin,* which means "burnt wine," an apt name since brandy is the result of heating wine and distilling the essence. It is then aged in barrels, or has caramel coloring added to give it the appearance of aging.

Brandy is also made from fruits other than grapes, in which case it is called "eaux-de-vie." Brandy has been around for hundreds of years, but rose to prominence in the 12th to 14th centuries. It is generally believed that originally wine was distilled as a way to preserve and reduce the volume for transport. The idea was to add water back before consumption, but it was discovered that storing and aging the wine is wooden casks actually improved the product, and it began to be consumed "as is."

Brandies are produced all over the world, and the many varieties are named specifically for the country or region they are produced in. All brandies are produced in a similar manner, and each country and region has its own classification system but the great French brandies, Cognac and Armagnac, are the benchmark by which most other brandies are measured.

[Image courtesy of www.bluekitchen.net]

<u>Cognac</u> is a variety of brandy from the Cognac region of southwest France. Some of the finest brandies in the world are produced here, following very strict regulatory controls. Aging is very important in the finished product, and there are several classifications to denote this. The minimum aging is two years, but some of the finest cognacs are aged for fifty years or more, and may cost thousands of dollars. During the aging process, alcohol escapes into the air at the rate of about 3% per year. This is called "the angel's share," and it is said that it is detectable in the air in the Cognac region of France. Cognac reaches its target alcohol volume of 40% in about 40 to 50 years. By this time the oak barrels have stopped contributing any flavor components, and the cognac is transferred to glass containers and stored for blending.

There are three basic grades of cognac:
- VS (very special), in which the youngest brandy in the blend is aged for a minimum of two years
- VSOP (Very Superior Old Pale), with the youngest brandy having been aged for a minimum of four years
- XO with the youngest brandy having been aged at least six years, but on average it is usually more like 20 years

Within these broad classes, we also have:
- *Napoleon,* which falls between VSOP and XO
- *Extra,* usually older than a Napoleon or an XO
- *Vieux,* another grade between VSOP and XO
- *Vielle Reserve and Hors d'Age,* both of which denote terms that producers use to market very high end product that exceeds the official age scale of Cognac grades.

The most popular brands of Cognac are Courvoisier, Martell, Remy Martin, and Hennessy.

[Image courtesy of www.misscharming.com]

<u>Armagnac</u> is another great French brandy, made from the grapes of the Armagnac region of Southwest France in the Gascony region. Armagnac is very similar to Cognac because the same grapes are grown in the same region and a very similar production and classification system is used. However, Armagnac production is even older than Cognac and a principal difference is that Armagnac is aged in

black oak barrels, as opposed to the Limousin oak barrels that cognac is age in. The flavors imparted by each type of wood are very different.

Other French brandies are usually named for the region in which they are produced. The term *fine* is used to describe brandies from regions other than Cognac or Armagnac, so you will find *Fine de Bourdeaux,* or *Fine de Champagne,* for example.

Other Brandies

Spain: Brandy de Jerez is the typical brandy from the Jerez region in Andalusia in Spain. This is the region where sherry is produced, and most Spanish brandy is made by the sherry houses. The wine is usually produced elsewhere in Spain and then shipped to Jerez for aging. They are typically heavy and fruity.

Germany: Brandies from Germany are typically light and fragrant. The most famous is Asbach Uralt, "the great brandy from the Rhine," in Germany; most of the grapes and base wines are imported from Italy and France for blending and aging.

Greece: Metaxa is a brandy made in Greece. It is actually made from a blend of wine, spirit, and herbs, and is rich and fruity. Some people would classify it as a liqueur, but if you order a brandy in Greece, what you will get is Metaxa. There are three grades, with a range of 3 to 7 stars on the label. It is much sweeter than Cognac.

Mexico: Brandy outsells tequila and rum in Mexico, and the most popular brands are Presidente and Don Pedro; in fact, they are the largest selling brandies in the world.

South American Brandies are usually confined to their regions of production. Pisco is a clear, raw brandy from Chile and Peru, based on the sweet Muscat grape. Although it is technically a brandy, it is usually treated like a white spirit, and mixed with a sour or fruit mix and served over ice.

American brandies have been produced since the 1880's, but there is a renewed interest these days. Due to the huge success of California winemaking, attempts to match the sophistication of French brandies are being made. The classic French wine grapes are being used and aged for two to twelve years.

Cocktails

Setting up and serving cocktails is a large part of your service duty on a yacht, and you need to learn at least a few basic recipes for each classification of spirits, including vodka, gin, rum, tequila, whiskey, and brandy, as well as common aperitifs and digestifs, along with the garnishes, tools and techniques required to create them. It is a considerable body of knowledge, and as with wine, you need to learn the vocabulary of terms, the ingredients, the skills, the methods of serving and the correct glassware required.

A cocktail is an alcoholic mixed drink that contains two or more ingredients, at least one of which must be a distilled spirit. Originally, cocktails were a combination of spirits, sugar, water, and bitters. Today, the term refers to almost any mixed drink that contains alcohol, including those that combine alcohol with any number of mixers, such as sodas, fruit juices, sugar, milk, honey, cream, and various herbs and fruits.

The first U.S. publication of a bartending guide that included recipes for cocktails in the United States was *How To Mix Drinks or The Bon Vivant's Companion* by "Professor" Jerry Thomas, in 1862. Today, there are many bartending guides available, including the wonderfully comprehensive *Drinks,* by Master Sommelier Vincent Gasnier; *Professional Bartending* by Adam W. Freeth; and the highly informative and entertaining *Drinkology* by James Waller, to name a few.

Allegedly, the first American cocktail party ever thrown was in 1917 in St. Louis, by a Mrs. Julius S. Walsh, Jr. During Prohibition in the United States (1920-1933), alcoholic beverages were illegal. However, where there is a will, there is a way. *Speakeasies* sprang up in society as a place where illegal cocktails were still consumed. Gin (albeit of lesser quality) rose in popularity and outpaced whiskey because it was cheap and easy to produce and did not require any aging before consumption.

Cocktails went out of vogue for many in the United States during the late 1960's when the use of recreational drugs, both legal and illegal, became popular. In the 1980's, cocktails again became popular, with vodka often replacing gin. Many of the more traditional recipes regained popularity in the 2000's, and even more recently with the popularity and success of different movies and television series, such as "Mad Men."

There is a great little book, called *The Art of the Cocktail Party*, by Leslie Brenner. It contains various recipes for drinks, hors d'oeuvres, and canapes, along with a lively commentary about the portrayal of the art of the cocktail in film and print. Even Emily Post was a fan of them; in her *Pocket Book of Etiquette*, she praises cocktail parties: "Cocktail parties are a popular form of entertainment. They require little preparation, are limited as to time, and you can entertain many more people in a smaller space."

Assorted Cocktail Tools

boston shaker   cobbler shaker   hawthorn strainer   jigger

long bar spoon   muddle stick   tea strainer   measure spoon set

[Image courtesy of www.galleryhip.com]

Chapter 6

Guest Services: Coffee and Tea

Beverages, coffee and brandy are typically a separate course all their own in formal meal service. However, in everyday terms, hot beverages are served at various times throughout the day by several methods and styles. As a yacht stew, you will be expected to know how to distinguish different kinds of coffee and tea; to know how to operate and care for different kinds of equipment for brewing and serving beverages; and to know basic recipes, techniques, and service rules for coffees and teas. It is a thoughtful gesture to offer some sort of cookies or biscuits whenever you serve a hot beverage.

Stews and the Art of Coffee

"Coffee should be black as hell, strong as death, and sweet as love." —Turkish Proverb

A Brief History of Coffee

Coffee has been enjoyed as a beverage for hundreds of years; its history can be traced back to the 13th century. It is generally believed that it was discovered in the Kingdom of Kaffa in Ethiopia and then spread to Egypt and Yemen in the 1500's. The earliest credible written evidence of coffee drinking comes for the Sufi monasteries in Yemen. From there it appears to have spread to the Middle East, Persia, Turkey, and North Africa before spreading to Italy, the rest of Europe, Indonesia, and the Americas.

Some of the first coffee houses opened in Istanbul in the 1500's. The coffee beverage was alternately banned and revered. When it reached Venice via trade with North Africa, its consumption was initially banned, however, in 1600 Pope Clement the VIII gave it the green light for Catholics and its popularity grew from there. The first European coffee house, apart from those in the Ottoman Empire, opened in Venice in 1645. The Dutch can be credited with giving it the nickname "Java" when they began the first successful European coffee plantation on their island colony of the same name. The Spanish planted coffee from Java in the Philippines; seeds from Brazil reached Hawaii in 1825, and the French introduced it to their IndoChina colonies in the late 1880's.

Coffee was introduced to America as early as 1668, as a result of Dutch traders bringing it with them to the West Indies. American coffeehouses became centers of social, political, and business interactions. The Boston Tea Party pushed coffee's popularity, making it the national drink—it was seen as unpatriotic to drink tea. Once ties with England were severed, it became more convenient to import coffee from the Dutch and French islands in the Caribbean. Over time, coffee from Latin American countries rose in popularity. Changes in technology, industrialization, and marketing policies further bolstered coffee consumption.

In the early 1960's the coffee industry lost ground to the soft-drink industry here in America. More recently, an interest in coffee from around the world has fostered the specialty coffee industry. With this came the popularity of traditional coffee beverages from other countries, especially Italy, Spain and France. In America, we have been inundated with coffee choices in recent years, thanks in no small part to business chains like Starbucks, Barney's, Gloria Jean's, and Dunkin Donuts. There are those who love Starbucks coffee and those who don't, but there is no doubt that the success of this chain's business and marketing plan helped to popularize specialty coffee. It may seem like coffee is just coffee, but there are differences in the roast, the brewing method and the technique.

Coffee Beans

There are two major varieties of coffee beans: Arabica and Robusta. Arabica is a higher quality bean, which is grown at higher altitudes; it has a subtle flavor and aroma. Robusta is a darker brew with strong flavor and it is Robusta that produces the crema in espresso.

The flavor spectrum of coffee beans will vary according to where the plants are grown. The overall climate and the weather during a particular growing season will account for variations in quality and quantity for a particular year.

The Roast

Roasting coffee transforms the chemical and physical properties of green coffee and brings out the flavor characteristics. Roasting causes the green coffee beans to expand and to change in color, taste, smell, and density. Unroasted beans contain similar acids, protein, and caffeine as those that have been roasted, but lack the taste.

The beans are shipped green to the roaster and then blended and roasted according to customer order. Beans roasted at lower temperatures are lighter and smoother than dark-roasted beans, which produce darker coffee with a stronger taste. Dark roasted coffees are not necessarily stronger than light-roasted coffees but the flavors have developed differently and they have different taste characteristics.

1 Cinnamon   2 Light   3 City/Medium   4 Full City
5 Dark   6 French   7 Italian

HEIRLOOM COFFEE, LLC
ROAST COMPARISON CHART
Copyright 2012
All rights reserved.

[Image courtesy of www.heirloom-coffee.com]

There are several common coffee roasts:

- Light Roasts: Light-bodied coffee
    o Cinnamon Roast: mostly commercial roast
    o Light City Roast
- Medium Roasts: Sugars begin to develop and add body to coffee
    o City Medium / Full City Roast
    o American Roast
    o Breakfast Roast
- Dark roast: Strong caramel and spice notes begin to develop
    o Italian Roast: oils start to be released; sweet, smoky flavor develops
    o French Roast: becomes less sweet, more smoky flavor develops

Decaffeinated coffee, which removes a minimum of 97% of caffeine, is made in two different ways:

- Swiss Water Method: beans are passed through a high pressure filter and soaked for up to 12 hours to remove caffeine
- Direct Contact Method: a food grade solvent is used to dissolve caffeine during a soaking process

The Grind

The roasted beans must be ground so that the hot water extraction can release the essence. The finer the grind, the more quickly the essence is dissolved. Although coffee can be ground and stored for a long time before it is brewed, premium tastes and aromas are produced from beans that are ground just before extraction. Once it is ground, the coffee starts to lose flavor to the atmosphere.

COFFEE GRIND		
Coarse	Large and chunky, similar to heavy kosher salt	Plunger Pot, French Press, Percolator, Vacuum coffee pot
Medium	Gritty texture with visible flakes like very coarse sand	Drip coffee makers with flat bottom filters
Fine	Getting finer, like table salt	Drip coffee makers with cone shaped filters
Extra Fine	Finer than granulated sugar	Espresso machines pump or steam
Turkish	Powdered with no grains like flour.	Ibik

[Image courtesy of www.katherines.com]

Coffee Types

Coffee service can be unique within a particular culture, depending on where it is served. Most cultures have rules about how and when coffee is served. You will be expected to know how to make coffee styles distinctive to particular traditions. Following are the basic coffee types. Keep in mind that they may be interpreted differently in various cultures. For example, in Italy cappuccino is normally served only in the morning, while here in America people drink cappuccinos, lattes, and other specialty coffees at all times of day.

Espresso is a concentrated beverage brewed by forcing a small amount of nearly boiling water under pressure through finely ground coffee. The high pressure extracts a high percentage of essences and caffeine. Espresso is a strong blend of Arabica and Robusta and is dark roasted and finely ground. A single serving is usually one ounce. It should be crowned with golden foam known as "la crema," which holds and preserves the "aroma." Because it is brewed under high pressure, acids are left behind in the grinds and only aroma is extracted.

There are several ways you may be asked to prepare espresso, but it is properly served in small cups and saucers designed to hold an ounce or two:

- Doppio – Double the amount of espresso and double the volume of water.
- Ristretto – "Short" = shorten the extraction time to reduce the water dispensed.
- Lungo – "Long" = single shot topped with 1 ounce of hot water; can be doubled.
- Americano – Single shot plus 5 ounces of water.

Breakfast coffees are roasted and blended specifically to provide a strong flavor with a lot of caffeine. Breakfast coffees are a blend of Arabica and Robusta, which are dark roasted but not as dark as espresso.

Afternoon coffees are traditionally lighter-tasting beverages than morning coffees. You might offer an Arabica coffee such as Colombian Supreme.

After-dinner coffees are to be served in the demitasse cups that come with sets of fine china as a digestif after dinner. Choose the best flavor available to savor with brandy. Examples include Jamaica Blue Mountain and Kona. When offered as a digestif, sugar is served, but milk is not offered. With the addition of milk, the coffee is then considered a food and the digestif qualities are altered.

Coffee and Espresso Makers

For hundreds of years, making a cup of coffee was a straightforward process. Roasted and ground coffee beans were placed in a pot or pan, to which hot water was added, followed by attachment of a lid to start the infusion process. Throughout the 19th and even the early 20th centuries, it was considered adequate to add ground coffee to hot water in a pot or pan, boil it until it smelled right, and then pour the brew into a cup.

Today, brewing coffee can almost be considered an art form when you consider all of the various techniques and gadgets we employ to produce a cup of java. Onboard a yacht, a stew needs to be skilled in a variety of methods of preparing coffee, including:

Automatic Espresso Maker

[Image courtesy of www.coffeeclassics.com]

Automatic Coffee Maker

[Image courtesy of www.amazon.com]

Filter Coffee   French Press

[www.blogpaverk.com and www.amazon.com]

Percolator
Boiling water is forced up over the grounds through a filter basket

[Image courtesy of www.prima-coffee.com]

While the filter coffee maker and percolator are common items you might own in your own home, an automatic espresso maker is special piece of higher-end equipment. The drinks produced by these machines are special because of the unique texture and the temperature of the steamed milk. When a barista steams milk, tiny air bubbles are created that give the milk a creamy, velvety texture. The temperature of the milk should be between 130 and 160 degrees to prevent scalding the milk, and it is essential to get the proper ratio of foam to steamed milk. A skilled barista can make artistic shapes and patterns while pouring the milk on top of the espresso. Frothing the milk properly can be the most difficult part of the process and it takes practice. Each machine is different, and the pressure that the machine produces is extremely important. A good machine can be very expensive and will produce perfect coffees, while other machines just will not make a good cappuccino no matter how masterful you become!

China Dishware Used for Coffee

Coffee service is broken down into different types of service according to different times of day. A full set of formal china will have several different sizes of cups for the different coffee service procedures. The largest cup in the set will probably be a breakfast cup; there will be a smaller cup for afternoon coffee or tea; and the smallest cup will be the demitasse. There may even be a hot chocolate cup in the service. The demitasse cup and saucer are not necessarily for espresso; any strong, high quality coffee, such as Kona or Jamaica Blue Mountain can be served as a digestif after dinner.

After dinner cup, coffee cup, and breakfast cup

[Image courtesy of mariettesbacktobasics.blogspot.com]

Specialty Coffee Recipes

One challenge you may frequently face is how and what someone may order, and knowing how to interpret and execute that order. If someone orders a "double white mocha with light whip," how do you translate that into classic coffee terminology, and what exactly does that mean? Many times people order the drink they prefer from their favorite local coffeehouse. They may be expecting you to know how to recreate a beverage that is a proprietary recipe containing flavored syrups or other secondary ingredients that you may not have on the boat.

Here are some of the more common specialty coffee requests you will receive:

Basic cappuccino: 1/3 espresso, 1/3 steamed milk, 1/3 foamed milk.

- Serve in a warm thermal glass mug that holds 6-8 ounces.
- Prepare the espresso first, brewing directly into the mug if it will fit under the machine, and if not, into a small stainless steel pitcher, like those used as individual creamers in restaurants and diners.
- Next, steam the milk in a larger stainless steamer cup.
- Using a spoon to hold the foam in, pour the milk to fill the glass to 1/3 from the top; then spoon in the foamed milk.
- Garnish with powdered or shaved chocolate or cinnamon. Ideally, it will have a nice layered look

Latte (**café latte** or **café con leche**): 1/2 espresso, 1/2 milk or 1/3 espresso, 2/3 milk, plus a bit of foam

- Serve in a warm thermal glass mug that holds 6-8 ounces.
- Prepare the espresso directly into a 6-8 ounce serving cup
- Add steamed milk.
- Spoon a very small amount of foam on top

Latte macchiato: 1/3 espresso, 1/3 cold milk, 1/3 steamed milk, bit of foam

- Serve in a tall glass with a shot of espresso
- Prepare the espresso
- Steam the milk then add to espresso
- Add the cold milk
- Top with a bit of foam

Macchiato dopio: 2/3 espresso, foam

- Serve in an espresso cup
- Prepare the espresso
- Top with a spoonful or two of hot foam

Espresso con panna: 1/3 espresso, top with whipped cream

- Serve in an espresso cup
- Prepare the espresso
- Top with a dollop or two of whipped cream

Other Variations:

    Café mocha is a basic latte to which chocolate syrup is added. It is topped with whipped cream and shaved or powdered chocolate or coffee beans.

    A **mochaccino** is a basic cappuccino with chocolate syrup, topped with whipped cream and garnished with shaved or powdered chocolate. A **hot chocolate** is made with steamed milk and chocolate syrup to taste, topped with whipped cream and chocolate syrup or powder.

    Iced cappuccino is made by pouring one shot of espresso over a tall glass of ice; add one-third cold milk, then one-third foamed milk, and top with whipped cream and chocolate powder or shavings. Pouring a shot of espresso over ice and adding chocolate syrup to taste makes an **iced mochaccino**. Fill with cold milk, top with foamed milk and then with whipped cream. Garnish with chocolate syrup.

Café au lait is the name for the French beverage that is a milder version of the Italian café latte. It is made in a 6-8 ounce mug or cup, consisting of one-half strong brewed coffee and one-half steamed milk. You can top it with foamed milk if you like.

Some other terms you might encounter include:

- **Breve**: Espresso with half and half
- **Caffe freddo**: Chilled espresso in a glass, sometimes over ice
- **Skinny**: made with non-fat milk
- **Dry**: made with only foam and no steamed milk
- **Wet**: made with only steamed milk and no foam

As you can see, there is a lot to know to be a barista, but that should not prevent you from making and enjoying a variety of coffee beverages. Every machine is a little different, so practice, practice, practice and pretty soon you will be making latte art along with the best of them!

[Image courtesy of www.mrcoffee.com.my]

Stews and the Art of Tea

"There are three things in life one will never master:
Tea, Tai Chi, and Tango." —unknown

The art of tea is a lifelong learning experience that takes not only careful discernment but also education of the palate.

As a stew, you will often find that your guests are knowledgeable about tea and tea drinking etiquette, so it's important to have a good knowledge of the various kinds of tea, how to make it and present it, and even some of its rather fascinating history.

There are many interesting books about tea, but my favorite is *The London Ritz Book of Afternoon Tea: The Art and Pleasures of Taking Tea* by Helen Simpson. It is small, but it has an interesting history of tea, numerous recipes for sandwiches, savories, cakes and scones, and appealing trivia and anecdotes about tea.

A Brief History of Tea

Tea plants are native to East and South Asia, probably originating in the areas of India, North Burma, China, and Tibet. No one is sure of the origin of tea being prepared as a beverage, but the first records of tea consumption are from China in about the 10th century BC., after which it spread to Japan and Korea.

In the early 16th century the Portuguese began to import tea, which they called "cha." Tea experts traveled from China to the Azores to cultivate the tea plant (camellia sinensis), along with jasmine and mallow to give the tea aroma and distinction. In 1660, Catherine de Braganza married Charles II and took a chest of tea with her to Britain as part of her dowry. Tea suddenly became all the rage at court. It was green tea, served without milk or sugar, in blue and white cups with no handles, and served from stoneware pots in the Oriental style.

Tea was a luxury item and very expensive, but for those who could afford tea and the paraphernalia that went with it, a treasured ritual was born. By the late 18th century, tea had become a national passion in Britain. It became accessible to all and had great popular appeal. Tea gardens sprang up, and anyone was allowed in if they paid an entrance fee. A noble lady could easily bump into her maid at one of these pleasure gardens. However, as the popularity of tea rose, tea traders came up with ways to undercut the prices. They invented a mixture called "smouch," which consisted of a blend of tea leaves, ash tree leaves, and sheep's dung. Eventually, the "tea bag" was invented to ensure top quality tea leaves without any illegal adulteration or additives.

In 1826, John Horniman was the first to develop the practice of placing a guaranteed net weight of tea in sealed packets, and other proprietors soon followed his lead. Horniman's business was eventually purchased by two orphaned teenage brothers whose name you may be familiar with today: the Tetleys. These young men made a small fortune selling tea to outlying districts around Yorkshire and Tetley tea continues to be a well-known and respected brand of tea today.

Interestingly tea did much to improve national health: 1) because it required the water to be boiled; and 2) because it began to replace cheap gin as the beverage of choice. As the popularity of tea continued to soar, it began to have a favored spot at temperance meetings, where it was encouraged that tea be taken instead of alcohol. To further make a statement, the tea at these meetings would be poured by a reformed drunkard.

As Britain became a nation totally obsessed with tea, China still controlled the tea trade and began to restrict trade with Britain. As a counter-measure, Britain began to invest heavily in the opium trade, which caused problems for China, and thus triggered the Opium Wars. When Hong Kong was ceded to the British in 1841, trade restrictions were lifted and more than 100 years of occupation by the British began.

In the meantime, tea had been discovered growing wild in India, and soon enormous quantities of tea were pouring into Britain from various corners of the British Empire. However, the British did not know how to produce tea as the Chinese did. In particular, they did not know how to stop the fermentation process and thus inadvertently produced black tea, which was much stronger and darker than the Chinese green teas.

Every year in the spring, the first tea buds to bloom are known as the "first flush." In the 1800's Queen Victoria was offered the "first flush" of black tea from the Darjeeling region near the Himalayas. It was thought to be the finest tea. To this day, the Queen still receives the first case of the first flush from the Margaret Hope Darjeeling plantation each year. Technically, it is more like a green tea than a black tea, similar to an Oolong.

The invention of "Afternoon Tea" is credited to Ann, the 7th Duchess of Bedford, who grew tired of the "sinking feeling" she experienced daily in the dull space of time between meals. In 1840, she began having a tray of tea, breads, and cakes brought to her room every day. Soon afternoon tea had become a national passion, fostering the production of elaborate paraphernalia and the establishment of rituals of etiquette to go along with it.

The favored hour for tea was 5 o'clock, and it became a lavish affair, complete with uniformed footmen and professional musicians. It was called "low tea" because it was generally served at a low table, like a coffee table.

Types of Tea

All true teas come from the same plant *camellia sinensis*, but there are thousands of varieties that make very different teas. You are probably familiar with the following broad categories of tea:

Green teas are unfermented tea. Green teas are mainly from China, Japan and Taiwan. They are the result of picking the tea and then stopping the fermentation by heating the leaves. This prevents enzymes from changing the nature of the tea.

Black teas are the result of withering and twisting the leaves so that they are oxidized by their own enzymes. They are either semi-fermented or fully-fermented. Semi-fermented teas are still black teas but are only fermented for a few hours to retain their flavor. The most famous semi-fermented teas are the Oolongs. Fully fermented black teas are very rare. Two famous examples are Lapsang Souchong and black Keemuns.

White teas are very lightly oxidized teas, in which the structure of the leaf cell is kept intact and not broken by the production methods used in other teas. The same leaves that are made to make white teas can be used to make green teas.

[Image courtesy of jungpanatea.wordpress.com]

Within these broad categories, there are thousands of varieties. The climate and location and soil all have a large influence on the flavor and style of tea. It is recommended to become familiar with the popular varieties of tea that you may come across:

Begin with the most basic level of Indian and Ceylon (renamed Sri Lanka after 1972) teas:

- Assam: A bold, brisk, bracing, strongly colored tea. This is what the British popularly expect from a cup of tea.
- Darjeeling: The "champagne among teas," this tea has a delicate wine-like flavor, often described as flowery or blackcurrant. It is lightly colored with a distinctive bouquet.
- Ceylon: These bright teas are grown at high altitudes, which have the best climate for growing teas. They turn a lovely golden color when milk is added.

Next, try the fine black teas of China, which are quite different from the first group and are part of a much more ancient tradition:

- Keemun: This is the tea of Imperial China. It is a delicate pale gold, with a light fruity taste, and the Chinese say it has a flavor like orchids. It can be taken with or without milk. It is considered by most to be the finest of all Chinese black teas.
- Lapsang Souchong: This is a tea that is either loved or hated. It has a heavy, smoky flavor with a specific pungency that is from the soil

where it is grown. It is a bracing, large-leafed tea that pours out a clear, bright color and is not taken with milk.

Other teas from China include the following well-known green teas. They are not taken with milk, but some people like to add lemon.

- Jasmine: This is a large-leafed, semi-fermented tea, scented with jasmine flowers. The flowers are often left in the tea, and they expand beautifully, releasing a lovely scent.

- Gunpowder: This is one of China's oldest teas. It is so named because its large, greenish-grey leaves are rolled into pellets resembling gunpowder. It is thin, pale, slightly bitter and straw-colored, and it has the lowest caffeine level of any tea.

- Formosa Oolong: A partially fermented tea with the delicate flavor of peaches, it is amber-colored and low in caffeine. It is grown on the island of Taiwan. There are actually many Oolong teas, but Formosa is the most famous.

Besides these particular types of tea, there are also many well-known, classic blends of tea including:

- Earl Grey: Named after the second Earl Grey in 1830, while he was Prime Minister under William IV; it is a blend of Chinese tea, Darjeeling tea, and oil of bergamot, which is a citrus fruit from the Mediterranean.

- Lady Londonderry: This tea was named after a popular British hostess in the early 1900's who was noted for her beautiful English gardens as well as her philanthropy and volunteer works during World War I. She had a particular blend created for her by Jacksons of Piccadilly. It contained Ceylon, India, and Formosa teas, and had a lemony, strawberry scent.

- Russian Caravan: A blend of Keemun, Oolong, and Lapsang Souchong, it is described as an aromatic, full-bodied tea with a sweet, malty taste. It was carried by camel caravan from China across the mountains and deserts of Asia to Russia, a journey of 6000 miles that took at least six months. It supposedly took on the scent of campfires, as well as a peculiar delicacy from being unloaded and placed on the snow-covered steppes while the travelers rested at night.

- English Breakfast: This is a full-flavored tea that is a strong, good quality blend of Indian and Ceylon tea.

- Irish Breakfast: This is an even stronger blend with a higher proportion of Assam.

Store loose tea in tins with insulated lids to protect it from humidity and air. Do not refrigerate or freeze. Most teas will last a year; second flush Darjeelings will last only 3-6 months.

[Image courtesy of www.amazon.com]

The Secrets of Brewing Tea

The larger the tea leaf, the longer it takes for the leaves to open and infuse. The smaller the tea leaf, the faster the flavor is released. The larger-leafed teas are called Pekoes or Orange Pekoes, and both terms refer only to the size of the leaf. These teas should be infused for 5-6 minutes. Smaller leaves or fannings (crushed pieces) take 3-4 minutes, and the smallest bits, called dust, release their flavor almost immediately.

To make tea:

- Fill a tea kettle with freshly drawn cold water; it is important to use fresh water because of its oxygen content. (Boiling for too long destroys the oxygen, and reusing water will affect the taste of the tea.)
- Put the kettle on the stove.
- Just before the water comes to a boil, pour some into your teapot to

warm the pot. Return the kettle to the stove and bring to a boil.

- While waiting for the kettle to boil, swirl the hot water around in the teapot until it warms to the right temperature and then pour it out. It is important that this first batch of water is just below boiling so that the water you add next, with the tea, stays at the boiling point, allowing the leaves to unfurl properly.
- Measure one heaping teaspoon of tea for each person plus one for the pot, and add to the teapot.
- When the water in the kettle is at full boil, pour it over the tea in the teapot. Allow to stand for the proper amount of time for the tea you have chosen, probably somewhere between 3 and 6 minutes.
- Give it a good stir and then pour it, using a strainer to catch the leaves. If you take milk with your tea, you should add it to the cup, cold and fresh, *before* pouring the tea.

tea brewing guidelines

Tea (2.5g)	Water Temp. (200ml water)	Steep Time
Green Tea	165-185 °F / 74-85 °C	1 - 3 min.
White Tea	160-175 °F / 71-80 °C	2 - 3 min.
Oolong Tea	185-200 °F / 85-93 °C	2 - 3 min.
Black Tea	205-212 °F / 96-100 °C	3 - 5 min.
Herbal (tisanes)	205-212 °F / 96-100 °C	5 - 8 min.

teaandallitssplendour.com

Do not leave the tea leaves in the pot longer than the recommended time for the type of tea you are using or it may become bitter. If you are using a tea ball or some other type of infuser, simply remove the tea at the proper time. If you are using loose tea that is not in an infuser of some sort, you can pour the tea into another warmed pot. Then you can cover the pot with a tea cosy and keep it bright and fresh.

Serving Tea

Afternoon tea is an English tradition dating back several hundred years to the times when landed gentry families would make social calls between 3 and 5 pm to chat and take tea. This genteel social event was usually called "low tea", because it was served on an elegant low table. The less affluent members of society often took "high tea", which was a sort of rough peasant meal consumed at the end of a long work day, served at a rustic high table to workers seated on high stools.

A tea menu includes traditional tea dishes, including a selection of cakes, cookies or pastries, and small sandwiches. Sandwich fillings may include chicken salad, smoked chicken or turkey, sliced baked ham, and the eternal favorite, cucumber sandwiches. The full tea experience consists of three courses served in the following order:

- Savories: little sandwiches or savory appetizer snacks
- Scones: served with Devonshire or clotted cream
- Pastries: cakes, cookies, shortbread, and sweets

When serving tea, place all of the service items on a table or tray. The table or serving tray should have the teapot, water pot, milk pitcher, sugar bowl, and waste bowl, along with a tea strainer and a small plate or bowl of sliced lemon. Offer white sugar and cold milk. Remember that green teas and jasmine teas are never taken with milk. It is acceptable to add very hot water to the pot and the tea will continue to brew; the second brew is better flavor than the first. If you are serving coffee, too, the coffeepot, cream pitcher, and sugar bowl should be set up separately on another tray or on the other side of the tea table.

Provide a teacup and saucer for each guest within easy reach of the person who pours. Arrange small plates, dessert forks, and napkins on one side of the table. Then arrange the cakes and sandwiches on plates or on tiered service piece. If there is room, you can place a small floral arrangement or other centerpiece. Candles are not appropriate at teatime, unless it gets dark very early.

For a small gathering, the hostess may want to serve the tea and food herself. At a large gathering, she may ask you or other guests to serve it. If you are going to pour the tea you must ask each guest whether they take milk or not. If they do, pour ½ inch of milk into the cup first.

Tea Service

[Image courtesy of brownpalace.com]

[Image courtesy of blog.williamhanson.co.uk]

[Image courtesy of spadge.uk.com]

[Images courtesy of www.rosesoveracottagedoor.com]

"There are few hours in life more agreeable than the hour dedicated to the ceremony known as afternoon tea."

—Henry James

Chapter 7

Guest Services:
Cheese, Caviar, and Cigars

Cheese service, caviar service, and cigar service may not be common in your everyday hostessing but they are quite popular upon yachting excursions.

Cheese Service

"I've never met a problem that cheese couldn't solve."
—A Wise Guy

A nice cheese tray makes a perfect mid-afternoon or cocktail hour snack, and stews should know how to put a cheese tray together quickly in case the chef is unavailable. Always be certain what cheeses you may have permission to use if the chef is absent. The chef has usually purchased the cheeses very carefully, and may have a specific meal menu in mind for each item. Always ask for permission, if you are not sure which cheeses you are allowed to use for an impromptu cheese tray.

Types of Cheese

There are several types of cheese, and within these types between 500 and 1000 varieties have been identified. Cheese is differentiated by moisture content and content or source of milk.

Cheeses vary from soft to hard; the amount of moisture in a cheese, the pressure used to pack the cheese and the length of time it is aged determines the hardness.

Semi-soft cheeses have a high moisture content and are often mild in flavor. Havarti, Muenster, and Port Salut are considered semi-soft cheeses. Some examples of denser semi-soft cheeses are Swiss, Emmental, Gruyere, Gouda, Edam and Jarlsberg. The eyes, or holes, in Swiss-style cheeses are created by bacteria, and this also gives them sharper, more aromatic flavors.

Harder cheeses, such as Cheddar, have a lower moisture content. They are usually packed into forms under higher pressure, and they are aged longer than softer cheeses. Cheddar cheese is actually named after the English village of Cheddar, but over time it has become a generic name. Cheddar cheeses are marketed according to flavor strength or the length of time they have been aged. Other cheeses that are similar but somewhat milder include Colby and Monterey Jack.

Hard cheeses, or grating cheeses, such as Parmesan or Peccorino Romano are firmly packed and aged for months or years.

Fresh cheeses are aged very little, and those without preservatives can spoil very quickly. They are the simplest cheeses to make. Basically, milk is curdled and then drained. They are soft, spreadable, and mild-flavored. Examples are cottage cheese, cream cheese, and fresh chevre or goat cheese. Ricotta is similar, but it is made only from whey, not from whole milk. Mozzarella is a fresh cheese made in the *pasta filata* style, which means that it is spun, stretched, or pulled before it is shaped into balls. The cheese is preserved in a salted brine. Traditionally from Southern Italy, it is often made from water buffalo milk. Water buffalo are not indigenous to the region, but were introduced in the 7th century to plow the fields south of Naples. At the end of World War II, most of the buffalo that were being used for Mozzarella production were slaughtered by the Nazis.

Part of the recovery effort after the end of the war involved importing water buffalo from India to build up the herds. Provolone is another example of *a pasta filata* cheese.

Cheeses are also categorized by content according to the source of the milk used or by added fat content. Milks commonly used for cheese include cow's milk, goat's milk, sheep's milk and water buffalo's milk. Some cheeses with the same name, such as feta cheese, may be made from the milk of different animals in different regions. For example, feta cheese is made from sheep's milk in Greece, while it may be made from cow's milk in other regions.

Triple cream cheeses contain at least 75% butterfat and are rich and creamy. Some are fresh, like mascarpone. Others are soft-ripened such as Boursault and St. Andre.

Soft-ripened or bloomy rind cheeses are exposed to mold in the aging process. They are firmer when they are younger, but ripen inward and become softer with aging. They are covered with a flexible white crust on the outside and have smooth textures and intense flavors on the inside. There are two common strains of mold used: *penicillium candida* and *penicillium camemberta*. Brie and Camembert are two examples of soft-ripened cheeses. The yeast develops a light furry covering of mold during aging.

Washed-rind cheeses also ripen inward as they age. They are washed in saltwater brine or a mold-bearing agent such as beer, wine, brandy, or local spirits, according to the traditions in each region. The washing cures the cheese and helps break down the curd from the outside, so it gradually becomes part of the cheese, not just a skin. The colorful, pungent exterior contrasts with the smooth and creamy interior. Examples include Munster, Raclette, and Epoisses.

Blue cheese is characterized by a distinctive blue vein pattern which is a byproduct of the production method. The cheese is inoculated with the bacteria penicillium glaucum. Since the mold needs oxygen to grow, whole cheeses are pierced with needles to allow air to enter. This allows internal as well as external "bluing."

Processed cheese is a food product made from normal cheese and various additives such as emulsifiers, salts, and food colorings. In America the most recognizable kind of processed cheese is American Cheese. The first commercially available sliced processed cheese in America was introduced by Kraft foods in 1950. It is popular for grilled cheese sandwiches and on cheeseburgers. The Laughing Cow brand is an example of a European processed cheese that is distributed in America.

Type of Cheese	Moisture Content	Texture	Shelf Life	Varieties
Soft Cheese	45 – 75 %	Soft, White, Spreadable	A few days	Cottage Ricotta Cream
Semi Hard	35 – 45 %	Firm, Crumbly, Can be sliced	A few months	Mozzarella Brie Camembert Swiss Edam Gouda
Hard	13 – 34%	Very firm, dense, sometimes grainy	One year or more	Parmesan Cheshire Cheddar Emmental Gruyere
Blue Vein	It has a network of green blue veins of mould throughout the body of the cheese.			Stilton Roquefort Gorgonzola

[Image courtesy of http://oer.nios.ac.in/wiki/index.php/Cheese]

Serving cheese

Cheese is always served at room temperature as it allows the full flavor of the cheese to emerge. This can take from 30 minutes to one hour. Hard cheeses take longer to come to temperature than soft ones. Unwrap the cheese to slice it before it gets too soft, then wrap it up again so the cheese does not dry out. Uncover it just before serving.

Use a good chef's knife to cut cheese properly. Fresh, soft cheeses can also be cut cleanly by using a piece of dental floss. Cheese must lie flat to be easily cut, and use a separate knife for each cheese.

To serve, place an assortment of cheeses on a flat tray or cheese board.

You may also use a piece of marble, a cutting board, or a plate. Allow a generous amount of space between the assorted cheeses so they don't run into each other and so the odors don't intermingle. This can make it hard to differentiate between them.

A typical assortment for a cheese tray:

- Bleu – With blue-green veins, tangy and sharp
- Port du Salut – Buttery textured, semi-soft cheese with a creamy yellow body
- Gouda – Semi-soft to firm with a mild nutty flavor
- Brie – Soft yellow with a mild, distinctive flavor
- Cheddar – Mild to sharp, white, yellow, or orange
- Chevre – Great with fresh olive oil drizzled over it and cracked black pepper

Dried cranberries, fresh apple, grapes and pears, and nuts are always good with cheese. Sliced sausages are another good accompaniment to fresh cheese.

[Image courtesy of finecooking.com]

Caviar

"Caviar is to dining what a sable coat is to a girl in evening dress." —Ludwig Bemelmans

Caviar service may be a simple or an elaborate presentation. Caviar is often served on special occasions, and is usually very expensive. The accompaniments of caviar service take some time to prepare, so be sure that the chef is given enough time in advance to prepare this service.

So what's the big deal about caviar? Caviar is often associated with luxury and wealth. While it is simple to serve, it can be very expensive. Caviar is the processed, salted roe—or eggs—of sturgeon. True, gourmet caviar comes from sturgeon only. There are many varieties of caviar, and it is important to understand how caviar is labeled. When buying caviar, you should know what species the caviar is, the country of origin, and the date of harvest. At one time the Convention for Trade In Endangered Species banned any export of caviar harvested from wild sturgeon from the Caspian Sea for several years. Today the majority of caviar types that are available are farm-raised.

At the beginning of the 19th century, 90% of the world's caviar came from the United States. Hudson River sturgeon were so plentiful, that it was served in saloons much like pretzels are today. It was also very common in California during the Gold Rush days. By 1910 lake sturgeon were nearly extinct and production stopped. Today, every species of sturgeon is on the endangered species list. The largest remaining population of sturgeon is in the Caspian Sea, formerly shared by Russian and Iranian producers. Since the breakup of the Soviet Union, the seven independent nations that border the Caspian Sea have been engaging in unregulated production.

Before the ban, the three main "classic" varieties of caviar available in the United States were Beluga, Osetra, and Sevruga. The most expensive was Beluga. The beluga sturgeon can reach well over one ton in weight, measure over 20 feet in length, and live for more than 100 years. Beluga caviar is completely banned from import into the United States now. Beware of caviar that is labeled to mislead you; anything labeled "beluga", "river beluga" or "Chinese beluga" is probably from a sturgeon species that is only distantly related to the famed species (Huso Huso) that was harvested from the Caspian Sea.

Osetra caviars are among the finest in the world and wild "Royal Osetra" was coveted by the Russian tsars. One of the most successfully farm-raised sturgeon species today, the Osetra sturgeon produces caviar that remains a favorite of caviar purists. Some of the finest examples of Osetra caviar available on the global market today come from cold-water farms in Germany and Israel. The Osetra sturgeon can range from 50-400 pounds, and be up to 10 feet in length. They can live for up to 50 years.

The last of the three classic caviar varieties is Sevruga. It is the most commonly found sturgeon species in the Caspian Sea, as well as being the smallest species, weighing up to 150 pounds and measuring up to 7 feet in length. Like Beluga, it has a buttery flavor, but it is richer and saltier. Its intense, unique flavor is highly valued. It is often less expensive than other varieties.

Varieties of Caviar

Caviar is rated in two ways: 1) the size and color of the eggs; and 2) the method of processing

The color is designated as: 000 for light caviar; 00 for medium caviar; 0 for dark caviar. The best caviar is generally considered to be beluga caviar, which can range from pale silver gray to black. It is followed by the small, rare, golden "Imperial" sterlet caviar that was once reserved for Russian, Iranian, and Austrian royalty. The medium-sized gray to brownish osetra ranks next in quality, and the last in the caviar ranking is the smaller, gray sevruga caviar. However, the most expensive caviars are priced by rarity, not by "taste." Individual tastes vary and the "tasting" is up to the individual.

There are four types of caviar according to processing methods:

- *Malossol* is the method preferred by connoisseurs. The name means "lightly salted," containing from 3.5 to 5% salt. This term can be used to describe any high-quality caviar.
- *Salted caviar*, also called "semi-preserved caviar," contains up to 8% salt. Higher salt content contributes to a longer shelf life, but the flavor may be compromised.
- *Pressed caviar* is made from too-soft, damaged, and overly ripe eggs. It is treated, highly salted, and pressed to a jam-like consistency. At one time it was the only method available for preserving caviar; and some connoisseurs prefer it because of its highly concentrated flavor and aroma.
- *Pasteurized caviar* is heated and vacuumed packed in jars. It has a much longer shelf life, however, both taste and texture may be affected.

There are numerous less-expensive alternatives to caviar. As supply and production have dwindled, the US and more than a dozen other countries have begun farming sturgeon to preserve both the species and the caviar industry. Commonly farmed varieties are: Osetra, Baerii, and White Sturgeon. For consumers, farming ensures consistent production of high-quality, lower-priced caviar that is not from endangered stock.

There are also many varieties of roe taken from lakes and rivers. Caviar that comes from other fish, such as salmon caviar or paddlefish caviar, must be designated as coming from a source other than sturgeon. They include:

- *Hackleback* – sweet, nutty and buttery flavors; firm with a rich, glossy black color; medium size.
- *Salmon caviar* – a favorite of sushi chefs. Bright orange color, large eggs with a distinctive popping quality in the mouth, and fairly intense flavor; considered a kosher food because salmon have scales.
- *Whitefish* – another favorite of chefs. Natural golden color, mild flavor; takes well to infusing with ginger, truffle, or saffron flavors; small grains and an almost crunchy characteristic.

Serving Caviar

In serving caviar, the simplest ways are still the best. Usually it is served cold in a small crystal bowl laid on a bed of cracked ice with a small spoon made of natural material, such as horn, mother-of-pearl, or wood used to serve.

[Images courtesy of www.flickr.com]

Caviar is frequently served with toast points or blinis and garnishes may include: crème fraiche, chopped egg yolks and egg whites, capers, and onion. Another popular dish is caviar pie, in which various types and grades of caviar and roe are arranged artfully in a decorative pattern on top of an interesting layered spread.

Note: For more information about caviar, visit Petrossian.com online. Here you will find the fascinating history of the two Armenian brothers, Malcoum and Mouchegh Petrossian, who introduced caviar to Parisians in the 1920's. Also noted for foie gras & pate, smoked sturgeon, rich chocolates, and fine coffees and teas, the name Petrossian stands for quality. Here is a quote from the website:

During the "années folles," known as the "Roaring 20s" in the United States, Paris welcomed exiled Russian princes, intellectuals and aristocrats with open arms, and Parisians quickly embraced all things Russian, especially the arts, ballet, the choreography of Diaghilev, and the music of Igor Stravinsky. Nonetheless, there was one thing missing from the Russian expatriates' lives: caviar. The French had yet to be introduced to this rare delicacy, a situation that the Petrossian brothers immediately set out to remedy.

The rest is history...

Caviar Varieties

Petrossian Beluga Imperial	Petrossian Special Reserve Osetra	Osetra Golden Imperial	Petrossian Sevruga Imperial	Sevruga Classic Gray
$5500/lb	$5455/lb	$3528/lb	$6500/lb	$3744/lb
$12241/kg	$12000/kg	$7760/kg	$13600/kg	$8126/kg

[Images courtesy of travelbeat.com]
[Image courtesy of caviarexpress.com]

Cigar Service

"Life's too short to drink bad wine or smoke poor cigars."
—Don Johnson

Even if it seems counterintuitive, the accumulation of vast sums of wealth and cigar smoking are inseparable. Fine cigars are treasured just as much as rare vintage wines. The honor of presenting, cutting, lighting, and storing fine cigars invariably goes to the stew.

Cigar Wrappers

A cigar's outermost leaves (or wrapper) come from the widest part of the tobacco plant. The wrapper determines much of the cigar's character and flavor, and as such its color is often used to describe the cigar as a whole.

[Image courtesy of Cigar Wrapper Color Chart c/o Wikipedia]

Over 100 wrapper shades are identified by manufacturers, but the seven most common classifications are as follows, from lightest to darkest (see illustration above):

- *Double Claro* – very light, slightly greenish (also called *Candela*, *American Market Selection* or *Jade*), achieved by picking the leaves before maturity and drying them quickly, with the color coming from the retained green chlorophyll. Formerly popular but now rare.

- *Claro* – very light tan or yellowish; indicative of shade-grown tobacco.

- *Colorado* – a distinctive reddish-brown (also called *Rosado* or *Corojo*).

- *Colorado Claro* – medium brown; includes Natural and English Market Selectio.

- *Colorado Maduro* – darker brown; often associated with the African wrapper from Cameroon, and the Honduran or Nicaraguan wrapper grown from Cuban seed.

- *Maduro* – very dark brown or black; primarily grown in Connecticut, Mexico, Nicaragua and Brazil.

- *Oscuro* – Very black (also called *Double Maduro*), often oily in appearance; has become more popular in the 2000s; mainly grown in Cuba, Nicaragua, Brazil, Mexico, and Connecticut.

Cigar Shapes and Sizes

Cigars are commonly categorized by the size and shape of the cigar, which together are known as the *vitola*. The size of a cigar is measured in two dimensions: its ring gauge (its diameter in sixty-fourths of an inch) and its length (in inches).

The most common shape is the *parejo*, also referred to simply as "coronas," which have traditionally been the benchmark against which all other cigar formats are measured. They have a cylindrical body, straight sides, one end open, and a round tobacco-leaf "cap" on the other end – which must be sliced off, and then cut a V-shaped notch in it with a special cutter or punched through before smoking.

[Parejo]

[Torpedo]

[Pyramid]

[Perfecto]

[Presidente]

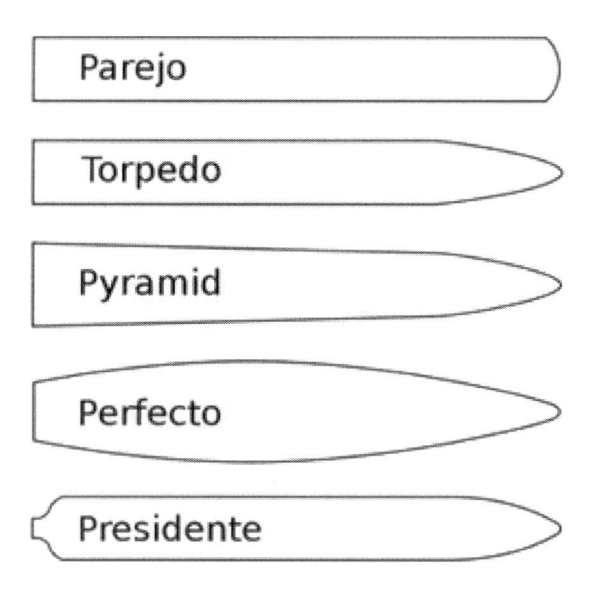

[Image courtesy of Cigar Shapes c/o CigarCrook.com]

- The *torpedo* shape cigar is like a *parejo* except that the cap is pointed.
- The *pyramid* cigar can be recognized by its broad foot, which evenly narrows to a pointed cap. The perfecto is narrow at both ends and bulged in the middle.
- The *presidente* or *diadema* is shaped like a *parejo* but considered a *figurado* because of its enormous size and occasional closed foot akin to a *perfecto*.
- The *tuscan* or *toscano* is the typical Italian cigar, originally created in the early 19th century when Kentucky tobacco was hybridized with local varieties and used to create a long, tough, slim cigar thicker in the middle and tapered at the ends, with a very strong aroma. It is also known as a *cheroot*, which is the largest selling cigar shape in the United States.

Cigar Storage

The undisputed first choice for storing and presenting fine cigars is in a "humidor." A humidor is a polished box lined with or made from cedar wood. It allows the cigars to breathe and, most importantly, it keeps them at a constant level of humidity of 70% at about 64-70 degrees F.

[Image courtesy of milantobacco.com]

Chapter 8

Food Safety

"Food safety involves everybody in the food chain."
—Unknown

Food safety onboard is extremely important and something that a stew always has to be aware of, whether we are working alongside the chef, preparing something for the guests, or dealing with food in any capacity at all. These are four basic tenets of food safety:

- **Wash.** Proper hand washing may eliminate 50% of all cases of food poisoning, and significantly reduce the occurrence of colds and flu. Hands should be washed in warm, soapy water before preparing foods and after handling raw meats, poultry, and seafood. Wash hands, wrists, fingers, and under fingernails thoroughly for at least 20 seconds—that's two choruses of "Happy Birthday." Always wash hands when switching tasks, from cutting produce to cutting meats, poultry, or fish. Dry hands with paper towels or air dry. Keep surfaces clean with warm soapy water and disinfect regularly with a bleach solution. Wash dishcloths and towels on the hot cycle of the washing machine. Replace sponges frequently.

- **Separate.** Keep raw meats and ready to eat foods separate. Be careful with cutting boards. Use two separate boards, one for raw meats, poultry, and seafood, and one for ready to eat foods like bread and vegetables. Dispose of cutting boards that have cracks and excessive knife marks from cutting and crevices, as these harbor bacteria. Store raw meats and poultry in bottom drawers of refrigerator so no juices drip down onto other foods. When preparing foods, wear latex gloves if you have a cut or sore on your hand.

- **Cook.** Cook foods to the proper temperature. Buy a food thermometer and use it. Learn the proper temperatures for each different food category. Calibrate your thermometer properly. Wash thermometer in warm, soapy water after each use

- **Refrigerate.** Refrigerate foods quickly and at the proper temperature. Foods should be kept below 40 degrees Fahrenheit to slow the growth of bacteria and prevent food poisoning. Leftover foods should not be left out more than 2 hours, and in weather with temperatures above 90 degrees, not longer than 1 hour. Make sure your refrigerator is kept below 40 degrees F to keep it out of the "danger zone." Keep a thermometer in your refrigerator at all times. Freezing is also a good option to extend the shelf life of perishable foods.

Expiration Dates

Any stew who has ever worked on a yacht knows how annoying it can be dealing with food and beverage inventories, expiration dates, and rotation. In simpler times, people survived without having expiration dates, "best if used by" dates or "born on" dates stamped on boxes, bottles, and cans; but these days, the amount of information we have to process is mind-boggling. Since we are usually responsible for beverages, crew snacks, and sometimes fresh food and dairy products, it's important to keep an eye on the dates and practice safe food hygiene, storage and rotation routines. This can save a substantial amount of time, energy, and money, as well as prevent any problems with food borne illnesses or food poisoning.

Always pay attention to the dates and markings on shelf-stable and perishable foods. However, if any food develops an "off" odor, color, or appearance, do not use it, regardless of the date on the container. If foods are mishandled, it is possible for food borne bacteria to grow rapidly and cause serious illness whether before or after the date on the product. This includes improperly thawed, stored, or cross-contaminated foods.

How long CAN we keep foods in stock before they become dangerous or harmful? In many cases, as long as they have been stored properly, unopened shelf-stable products like canned goods and dry foods will not become dangerous or harmful for a very long time, although they may lose flavor and potency. And "stored properly," in most cases, means without exposure to high humidity and temperature. Good luck with that, living on a boat!

Dating Systems

There is no uniform or universally accepted food dating system in the United States, and some states do not require a dating system at all. In fact, only 20 states require any food dating, with the exception of baby formula and some baby foods. Many of these systems are useful for providing marketing data and to increase sales for retailers.

What types of foods are dated, and what kinds of dating systems are used? Open dating systems use calendar dates, rather than a code, stamped on the product. It helps the store to determine how long to display a product for sale, and it helps the purchaser to know the time limit for best quality. You should buy the food before the date expires but it is not a safety date; if the food is stored properly it should still be safe to use for some time after that date passes. Similarly, if an item has a "best if used by" date, follow that date to ensure best flavor or quality; it is not a purchase or safety date.

On the other hand, if the item has a "use-by" date or no date, there are more specific rules that apply. This often refers to perishable goods such as meat, eggs, dairy products, and poultry. A "use-by" date is determined by the manufacturer and ensures that the food is safe and at peak quality as long as it is handled properly after purchase.

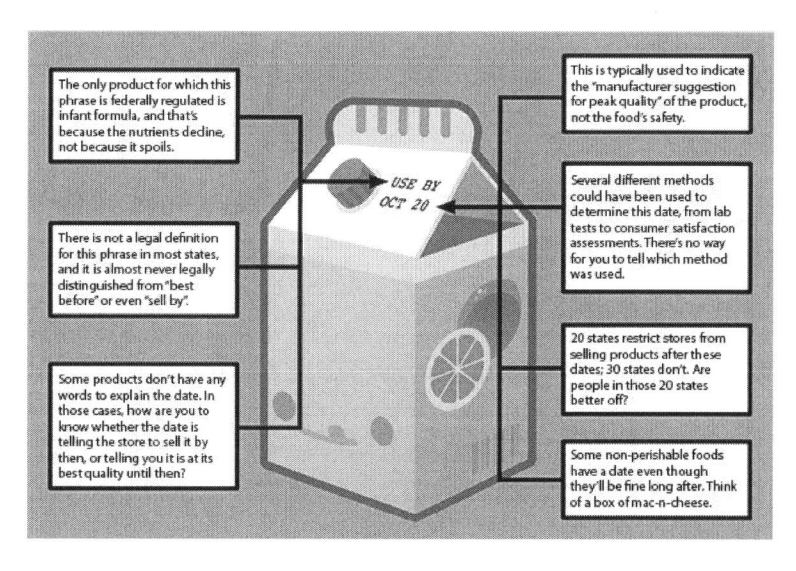

[Image courtesy of http://www.nrdc.org/]

Canned foods have particular codes stamped on them that refer to the manufacturing process. They are required for tracking foods in interstate commerce, in the event of a recall. They aren't meant to be interpreted as "use by" dates. Bar codes are used by manufacturers to track inventory and marketing, and do not have anything to do with tracking in the event of a recall.

- Canned food is processed in air-tight containers and should be fine for 12-18 months. However, if the can is dented or rusty, this indicates it has been punctured at some point which could speed up the process of spoilage.

- Foods like beans and vegetables are low in acid, so they actually may last for 2-5 years unopened.

- Higher-acid foods like tomatoes and pineapple should last for 12-18 months.

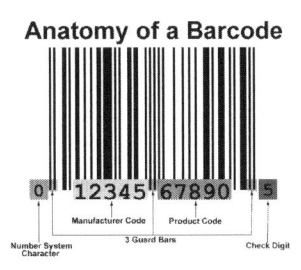

[Image courtesy of www.forbes.com]
[Image courtesy of www.cidyjufun.blogpot.com]

How long is long enough?

Refrigerator storage of most fresh or uncooked products varies, but in most instances it is best to freeze the item in question if it is not going to be consumed by the "use by" or "sell by" date, or if it has no date.

- Poultry and ground meats: 1-2 days
- Beef, veal, pork and lamb: 3-5 days
- Cured cook-before-you-eat ham: 5-7 days
- Eggs: 3-5 weeks
- Processed refrigerated products sealed at the plant, such as cooked poultry and cooked sausage: 3-4 days unopened, 3-4 days after opening
- Dried, shelf-stable sausage: 6 weeks unopened, 3 weeks after opening
- Bacon, hot dogs, and luncheon meat: 2 weeks unopened, 3-7 days after opening
- Canned ham labeled "keep refrigerated" is good for 9 months before opening

Common spices like salt and pepper will not expire in the traditional sense, as long as they are not exposed to moisture; they just become less and less flavorful. Within 2 to 4 years, most spices will lose potency and flavor and need to be replaced.

Cereals and crackers definitely go stale quickly, but they usually do not become harmful or toxic because there is not enough oil or moisture in them to grow bacteria or mold. They have been called "edible cardboard," and unopened could last 2-4 years without the safety and nutrient quality changing. The texture and taste will deteriorate, however, and may make them stale.

Just like cereal and crackers, dried pasta and rice do not contain enough moisture to promote the growth of bacteria and mold. They can usually safely be consumed for at least 2 years if unopened. Brown rice and whole wheat pastas may contain more oil, so they may not last that long. Again, the deterioration of texture and taste may determine how long you want to keep things around.

Condiments like ketchup, mustard, most salad dressings, pickles, horseradish and even mayonnaise can last up to a year unopened. Even after they are opened, they will last a long time. However, the gunk that accumulates around the top of the jar is not only unsightly; it is also the perfect place to harbor bacteria. Get in the habit of wiping tops of jars clean with a paper towel, and wash and dry the lids from time to time.

Honey does not spoil, but once the jar is opened it will begin to crystallize and lose its texture. Honey stays good for up to 12 months, whether it is opened or not. When the texture starts to change, it is probably losing its sweet taste as well, so maybe it is time to pitch it.

Sodas have a longer shelf life than most people realize, with the exception of artificially sweetened, sugar-free drinks. Artificial sweeteners break down quickly over time, and even more quickly if they are exposed to heat. Storing sodas on deck in 90 degree heat is not the best option, but often it is the only one we have, so plan to dispose of expired drinks regularly.

Most yachts are meticulous about rotating and inventorying the food they purchase, and with good reason. Food is expensive, and it would not do to present anything less than the highest quality food onboard. Pantries and food storage areas should be cleaned and organized regularly. Refrigerators and freezers should be kept as clean and hygienic as possible. It is always a good idea to have an inventory and rotation system in place.

Chapter 9

Housekeeping, Cleaning & Laundry

"Housekeeping is like being caught in a revolving door."
—Marceline Cox

Cleaning and Housekeeping

Every yacht is unique, but there are cleaning, housekeeping & laundry, and maintenance concerns that you will be responsible for on every yacht. You will need to know the specific check list and cleaning routine for all area zones including guest and crew cabins, crew mess, salons, dining areas, captain's cabin and other areas of the yacht. Knowledge of each of the items, surfaces, finishes and materials that you will encounter onboard is essential. As part of cabin day service and turn down service, you will need to know when and how frequently to do the tasks that are required to keep the interior running smoothly. Your schedule will cover what needs to be done daily, weekly, monthly and seasonally, and it will take several hours each day to clean the boat.

Housekeeping is somewhat of a lost art, but as a yacht stewardess you will become an expert housekeeper in no time, whether you aspire to or not! You will learn how to create a comfortable, safe and beautiful environment and know how to take care of everything within it. A large portion of your housekeeping skills will be devoted to maintaining, preserving and protecting the yacht furnishings, interior surfaces, interior fabrics, valuable art, collectibles, and decorative items. You will learn to care for marble, ceramics, wood, silver, brass, and gold. For example, many of the surfaces of bathroom fixtures on a yacht may be plated with gold, and you must learn how to protect and take care of these and all surfaces properly.

In addition to dusting, vacuuming, cleaning windows, scrubbing bathrooms, and caring for extremely valuable art pieces, you will spend a lot of time with upholstery, carpets, and fabrics. In particular, a great deal of your time will be devoted to caring for bed linens, table linens, and fine clothing made of cotton, linen, silk, bamboo, modal, suede, leather, cashmere and various synthetic fabrics. There may be a fortune's worth of expensive clothing, shoes, and accessories onboard, and you must know how to care for all of these items. Wardrobe management, packing and unpacking for guests, and valet services will be a part of your job.

Every yacht is unique, and you must know the proper way to care for each of the specific materials and furnishings on your particular yacht. It is important to educate yourself about the proper care of fine furnishings, artwork, and possessions. There may be a manufacturer's handbook available from the construction of the yacht which outlines care instructions for the interior surfaces and furnishings. If not, there are some excellent reference books you can consult. Martha Stewart's *Homekeeping Handbook* is a terrific overview and introduction of basic care for practically everything in every room of a house or yacht.

When it comes to taking care of expensive and rare articles, *Caring for Your Family Treasures* by Jane S. Long and Richard W. Long of the Heritage Preservation is a wonderful museum-conservator's-level guide for how to care for everything in the home, ranging from books, manuscripts, scrapbooks, and papers to paintings, fabrics, furniture, watches, ceramics, jewelry, metals and toys. There are even chapters on insurance, security, and information on where to buy supplies for cleaning and storage. This book is a good first step in understanding and dealing with valuables on the boat; however, it is imperative that you talk to the art dealers who provided the art pieces as well as the insurance representatives who provide coverage for the yacht to be sure that you are doing all of the right things.

Art Collections

Some yacht owners are also fine art collectors, and it is not uncommon for them to showcase their artworks on board the vessel. Many of the items you will encounter onboard are museum quality, treasured objects. It is easy to damage these delicate, expensive furnishings and items. Crew must know how to care for, secure, and insure fine art. The environment has to be controlled, especially humidity, so if something goes wrong with the cooling system, or you are going into a yard period, you might want to consult an expert to see about having major artworks removed and properly stored. If you do decide to have the art removed by professionals, make sure the right insurance coverage is in place before anything leaves the boat.

When new art is purchased, be certain it is documented correctly and that proper care instructions are understood by interior staff. Most oil paintings have a varnish coating and certain cleaning chemicals can damage them. Framed pieces under glass should only be lightly dusted, and any marks on the glass carefully removed. Do NOT spray cleaners directly onto the glass, because it can seep under the edges and destroy the painting. If any artwork is accidentally damaged, consult an art restorer to take care of it immediately.

Furnishings

Every yacht is unique. Due to the fact that you will have different criteria for cleaning on each one, it is beyond the scope of this book to go into detail about all of the rules of cleaning and maintenance, but you must educate yourself. Part of your job as a stewardess is to protect and preserve all items found on the boat. You will have to create a system for cleaning and maintenance task systems and schedules. A detailed guide for housekeeping is *Home Comforts: The Art and Science of Keeping House*, by Cheryl Mendelson. This will teach you the science of housekeeping. Thanks to the internet, there is exceptional access to information and products that are available to help you care for items correctly. The challenge lies in finding the right information and the safest materials to use so that you do not damage items.

On most yachts, there are far too many harsh chemicals for cleaning, and one of the surest ways to damage fragile surfaces is to use harsh chemicals! Many times the least harmful chemicals will be the simplest ones: water alone, pH neutral soap and water, or vinegar and water. Essential oils are another good option for making your own cleaning and disinfectant products.

If you have a large collection of precious items and valuable art objects onboard, it may be worth your while to contact a professional conservator – an expert in caring for objects placed in the public trust. Their expertise is based on scientific knowledge regarding how objects deteriorate over time and, conversely, how to protect them from deterioration.

Another good way to gather information is by conversing with craftsmen who are building, working on, repairing, or refinishing items on your boat. These people are professionals who know the qualities and attributes of the materials they are working with, and they often have a fierce passion for their craft. Respect their work, their knowledge, and their craftsmanship, and you will be suitably rewarded when you need help or guidance! A good motto for a stew is "leave the boat in as good as or better condition than when you joined the crew."

Table Linens

A large part of your job as a stewardess requires setting and decorating tables for meal service. You will be designing table décor for three meals every day when there are guests on. Table linens are the "canvas" upon which you display your table setting skills. Selecting table linens can be confusing because there are so many sizes and fabrics to choose from. Use this section as a helpful guide when dressing the table.

Size

For tablecloths, the drop length is an important consideration. This is the amount of fabric that hangs down over the edge of the table. Your tablecloth should hang down 6-8 inches on each side of the table. The longer the drop length, the more elegant the table.

Tablecloths come in standard sizes or you may have them custom-made. For a rectangular table, measure the length of your table plus two times the length of the drop you want. Compare your measurements against the measurements of the standard size tablecloth. If the measurement falls somewhere in between, go for the larger cloth.

Shape	Size	Fits table size	Seating
Square	52" x 52"	25" x 28" to 40" x 40"	4
Oblong	52" x 70"	28" x 46" to 40" x 54"	4 - 6
	60" x 84"	36" x 60" to 48"x 72"	6 - 8
Oval	60" x 102"	36" x 74" to 48" x 90"	8 - 10
	*60" x 120"	36" x 94" to 48" x 104"	10 - 12
	*60" x 144"	36" x 118" to 48" x 130"	12 - 14

*If you cannot find an oval cloth in the pattern selected, you can use an oblong size.
*Oval not available in all styles.

Round	70"	44" to 60" diameter	4 - 6
	90"	60" to 78" diameter	6 - 8

[Image courtesy of tableclothshq.com]

For placemats and napkins, you'll want a variety of shapes and sizes that coordinate with the dining areas of the yacht, the china and service styles, and the general decorating scheme of the yacht. They are available in numerous styles, materials and fabrics. (See Chapter 5 for more details)

[Image courtesy of Top Notch Tabletop]

White, off white, and ivory are considered the most formal colors. When choosing colored linens, you should select a color that complements the color of your dinnerware and the colors in the room.

Your linens should provide a color base for your dinnerware and centerpiece and not be the focal point of the table. Printed linens tend to be the most informal and look best with solid color plates and simpler flatware. Whatever you decide, don't be afraid to break out of the mold and be creative with your table designs.

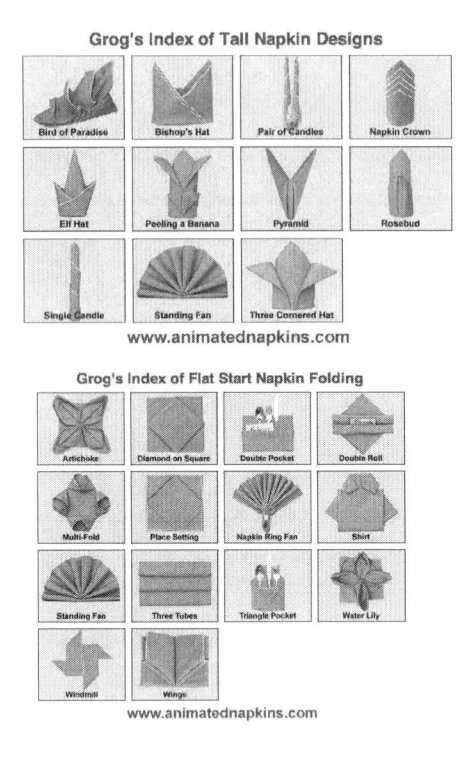

[Image courtesy of www.animatednapkins.com]

Types of Table Linen Fabrics

Table linens are very heavily used on a yacht. A stylish table setting is required for three meals every day. The tablecloths, placemats and napkins are laundered after each use, and quality really matters.

Table linens made from **cotton or linen** are preferable and generally last longer than those made with a synthetic blend. Linens made from **synthetic fabrics** may be less likely to absorb stains and often do not require ironing, but they lack the fine finish, hand feel, and durability of high quality natural fabrics. **Egyptian cotton** and **Irish linen** are considered the best fabrics for linens because their long, durable fibers don't pull and the fabric does not become shiny after ironing. **Damask-woven linen** and **cotton** are considered the most formal fabrics.

[Image courtesy of mapplique.com and italianfinelinens.com]

Table Linen Care

Follow the manufacturer's instructions for laundering and ironing all fabrics. Most stains from food, drink, and lipstick can be removed if the stains are pre-treated with stain remover and the linens are soaked overnight. A good stain removal guide is essential. In many cases, it is better to treat stains with common household products and old-fashioned remedies instead of strong chemicals.

A Few Rules

- Always treat stains as soon as possible; they're much easier to remove that way.

- When using things like lemon juice, alcohol, or vinegar, do a small test on the fabric in an unnoticeable spot to test color fastness.

- **NEVER** mix bleach and ammonia together.

[Image courtesy of www.maids.com]

Most table linens can be washed in warm or cool water with regular laundry detergent, but be sure to check the care tags on the fabric to avoid costly mistakes. Table linens with lace, cutwork, or delicate embroidery require special attention, and it may be easier to get them dry-cleaned. If you are not sure about the composition material of linens, *do not* put them in the dryer. For cases when you are certain it is safe to do so, place linens on a low dryer setting, then remove before they are totally dry to prevent excessive wrinkling. Iron and stow properly until needed. Note: cotton and linen tablecloths, napkins, and runners frequently need to be ironed again before use to make them crisp, even though they were ironed before they were put away.

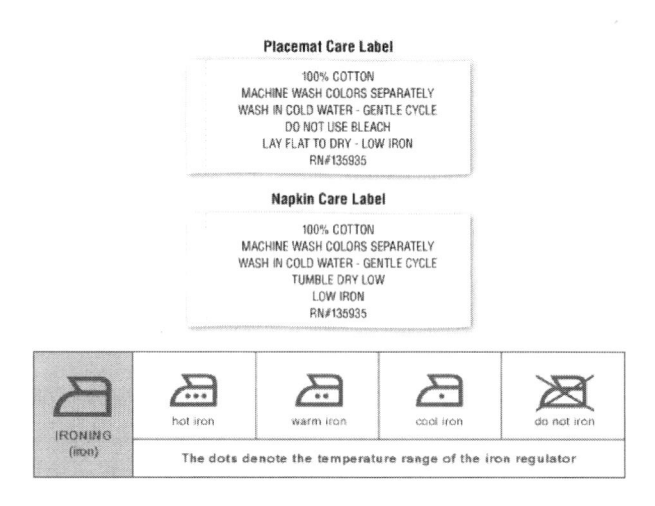

Placemat Care Label
100% COTTON
MACHINE WASH COLORS SEPARATELY
WASH IN COLD WATER - GENTLE CYCLE
DO NOT USE BLEACH
LAY FLAT TO DRY - LOW IRON
RN#135935

Napkin Care Label
100% COTTON
MACHINE WASH COLORS SEPARATELY
WASH IN COLD WATER - GENTLE CYCLE
TUMBLE DRY LOW
LOW IRON
RN#135935

IRONING (iron)	hot iron	warm iron	cool iron	do not iron

The dots denote the temperature range of the iron regulator

[Image courtesy of amazon.com]
[Image courtesy of french-handlaundry.com]

Bed Linens, Pillows, and Readying for Guests

Bed linens are a significant and expensive item for creating ambiance and exhibiting the decorating style on a yacht. Top quality bed linens are a considerable investment, and they require special care. They are available in many different colors, patterns, fabrics, and prices. It is important to follow the manufacturer's directions for care.

Buying Bed Sheets

You will need at least two sets of sheets for each bed; double that if the yacht does charters and you want to keep the owners' and charter sets separate. First, be sure to identify the correct size of the bed. The sizes available are: twin, double/full, full/queen, queen, king, and California king. It will be helpful if you have the actual measurements of each bed to refer to when buying sheets. On boats, beds are often sized to fit into a particular space and their measurements may not match exactly with manufacturers' dimensions.

Since it is not unusual to have several different sizes of beds, it is not unusual to have several different styles of sheets. Having sheets custom-fitted to the beds at the time of purchase is very helpful and efficient in the long run and is well worth the extra cost. For unusual and awkward bed configurations, it saves lots of time and energy to have the top sheets as well as the bottom sheets custom fitted. All sheets should be labeled for the port and starboard cabins they belong in, and for whether they are inboard or outboard beds, in order to eliminate confusion and frustration.

Flat sheets are not very difficult to deal with, but fitted sheets are another story. Fitted sheets come in different styles: those with elastic all the way around the sheet, those that have elastic only at the corners, and different pocket depths to fit standard and deep mattresses. If the pockets are too deep for the mattress, they will not fit properly. When you identify the style of the sheet, you will find the technique that works best for ironing and folding them.

Make sure you have enough pillowcases to cover all the pillows that will be put on the bed and that you have enough decorative shams to match each set of sheets. Pillowcases tend to need changing more often than sheets and they wear out more quickly, so have enough extras for backups, and rotate their use properly.

Cotton is the fabric of choice for bed sheets. It breathes easily and is soft against the skin. There are different types of cotton to choose from. Egyptian cotton is very soft and usually quite expensive. Pima cotton is grown in the southern U.S. and is soft and durable. There are polyester/cotton blends available that are less expensive but these are not as comfortable.

Thread count is another important consideration. The thread count number is the number of threads per square inch on the sheets. The higher the thread count, the finer the threads used, and the softer the sheets will feel. Keep in mind that higher-thread count sheets will be more expensive and may require more care. Thread count alone should not be the determining factor in choosing sheets. A high quantity thread count does not necessarily mean a high quality thread. Top quality sheets are usually in the 200-600 thread count range, and will have high quality fibers, yarn size, finishing, and construction.

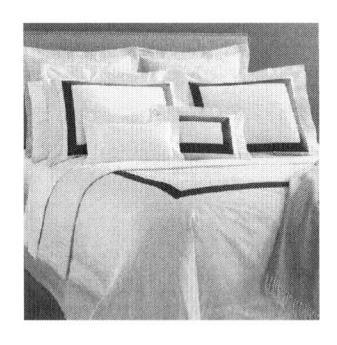

[Image courtesy of wayfair.com/sferra]

Caring for Bed Sheets

Bed linens are very expensive and require considerable care. Avoid using bleach on bed linens, because it breaks down fibers. Don't over-load the machines. Remove linens from the dryer while very slightly damp to reduce wrinkles and cut down on ironing time. If sheets have cooled in the dryer and wrinkles have set, toss a clean, dampened cloth into the dryer and run the dryer for another 5-10 minutes. Remove from the dryer and fold if they cannot be ironed promptly.

On many yachts it is recommend that you iron the sheets on the bed. You will most likely be ironing them for turndowns every night and again when you make the bed up in the morning.

Launder mattress pads regularly and have a extras for backup.

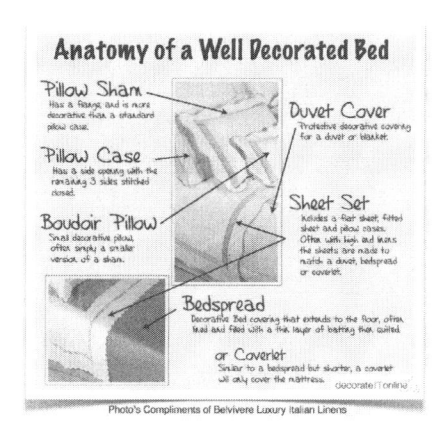

[Image courtesy of Belvivere Luxury Italian Linens]

Bed Pillows

Bed pillows are a very personal item and can be very expensive. High quality down and eiderdown can cost several hundred dollars apiece. Typically, the pillows on the boat are chosen at the same time as the bed linens. The owners and decorator will research products and then make the decision on how much money will be spent on pillows.

Deciding on the right size pillow:

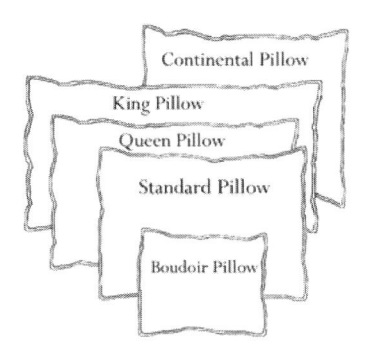

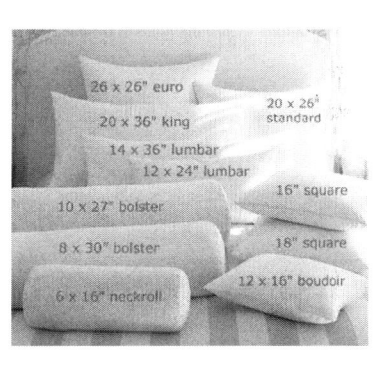

[Image courtesy of finelinenandbath.com]   [Image courtesy of atticmag.com]

The pillow size will depend on the size of the bed and how the person sleeps. For a twin bed, you would probably choose a twin pillow, but some prefer a queen or even a king pillow on a twin bed. For a queen bed, you would probably buy 2-4 queen pillows, and for a king you would buy 2-4 king pillows.

Determine your pillow budget: An inexpensive foam pillow may sell for as little as $5.00 but a top quality down or feather pillow can be hundreds of dollars, depending on the size. Sometimes it makes sense to select a mix of expensive pillows and some less expensive ones. Guests' preferences vary, so if you have extra storage space it is a good idea to have more than one style for them to choose from.

Choose the fill: A foam pillow will feel firm and hold its shape through the night, even when the person shifts on the bed. A down pillow will provide a soft cushion for the sleeper's head. A polyester filled pillow will be somewhere between a foam and a down pillow. A good quality compromise might be a pillow with a core of foam or feathers, surrounded with an outer coat of down. Most top-quality down pillows are hypoallergenic and can be used by people with allergies.

Soft or firm?: The volume of fill the pillow contains determines the "loft." For a firm pillow, the fill will be tighter. For a soft pillow, the fill will be lighter. Regardless of the firmness, feather and down will have to be replaced every few years and foam will disintegrate or break down.

Bed pillow cover and ticking: The cover of a foam bed pillow is not that important. For a down pillow, be sure that the ticking or cover is tightly woven cotton so that the feathers don't come out. Buy a washable pillow protector for every pillow. This will keep the ticking clean and protect the pillow cover.

Care of pillows: Clean bed pillows regularly. The pillow should come with care instructions. Some feather and down pillows can be washed in a washing machine. Others should be dry-cleaned. Take note of the cleaning instructions that come with the pillow.

Making the Bed

- The mattress pad goes on first; smooth it outward from the middle of the bed.

- Put the fitted bottom sheet onto the bed. Pull the elastic tightly and evenly over the mattress, working diagonally from one corner to the next.

- Add the top sheet by unfolding it, **with the printed or "right" side facing down**, the wide hem at the top, and the narrow hem at the bottom. This allows the right side of the sheet to show correctly when you fold down the top over the blanket. Spread the sheet out evenly across the bed and tuck in the bottom edge.

- Create the famous "hospital corner." Pick up the side edge at the bottom corner of the flat sheet and hold it out while simultaneously tucking in the part hanging down at the corner. Then let the edge fall and tuck it in at a 45 degree angle. Repeat this process at the other bottom corner. Alternatively, you can make a 90 degree angle on either the side or the bottom of the bed.

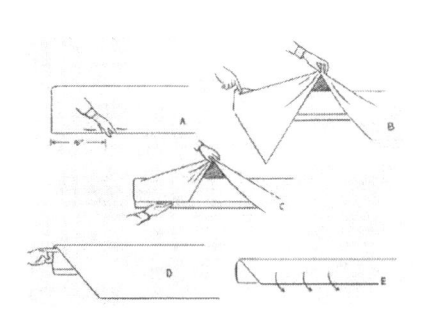

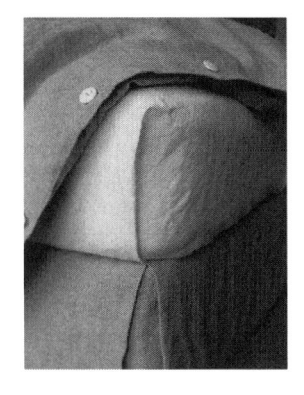

[Image courtesy of the artofmanliness.com]

- Put the blanket over the sheets. Place the blanket right side up with the top of the blanket at the point you wish to turn down the top sheet, usually about 6-8" inches from the top of the bed. Tuck in the bottom edge and make hospital corners there also.

- Fold down the top sheet over the edge of the blanket and then tuck in the sides. Sometimes another flat sheet is placed over the blanket.

- Finally, decorate the bed with a comforter, duvet, or bedspread. Add pillows, accessories, and any additional pillows on top.

Turn-down Service

Part of the 5-star luxury service a stew provides for guests onboard is the turn-down service. Turn-downs are usually done while the guests are having dinner or out for an evening meal. The practice involves removing and stowing heavy comforters and pillows, and then turning back the sheets and blanket on each side of the bed with a decorative fold and ironing the sheets and pillowcases so they look crisp and inviting.

Turndown service also includes checking and cleaning the room and bathroom one last time for the day so that everything is tidy and organized.

Last but not least, an important aspect of this ritual is leaving a surprise for guests to enjoy. For example, flower petals or a sweet treat can be placed on the pillows. Of course, one of the most common treats is a beautiful piece of chocolate. Keep in mind, however, that treats can sometimes prove to be impractical. Rose petals can stain sheets and chocolates can melt on the pillows if the guests do not remove them! The latest trend is customized turn-down items and you can get ideas for these at www.aqualuxeoutfitting.com and at turndown-cards.com.

If there are parents with small children onboard, the chief stew may want to check with the parents prior to the first evening turn-down to establish when and how to do turndowns.

Housekeeping Basics

There are different kinds of cleaning that you will be expected to know when working on yachts. Daily cleaning and dusting are different from what is called "detail cleaning." Detail cleaning is very particular and concentrates on cleaning, polishing, waxing, and buffing all surfaces in each area of the boat. You have different issues to deal with than in a home—salt in the air, exhaust in the air, a damp environment and often extreme heat and humidity if the air conditioning is reduced in the shipyard.

The vessel safety and integrity is your responsibility. It is your job to protect the interior. One of the most important things to remember is to know your materials and surfaces and do not cause damage to fine finishes. Make sure you understand what cleaning tools and supplies are safe to use onboard. Many products you will find onboard are very strong and abrasive. Materials onboard are expensive and likely to be more delicate than what you are used to at home. Have access to professionals for help and advice.

Learn about the artwork and decorative items onboard, and the proper way to care for them. Know how to protect artwork. Know when to call in an expert or an art conservator. Be aware of any insurance requirements before you remove anything from the vessel.

Know which areas of the vessel you are required to care for—which rooms, fixtures (heads, showers, drains, laundry equipment, appliances, etc. Work with hygiene in mind. Have a system in place for using proper types of cloths and sponges for wiping up specific areas. Wash separately or dispose of properly. Do not use guest towels for cleaning to avoid cross-contamination and to prevent damaging expensive guest amenities.

Always read and follow the instructions on cleaning products to know the proper amount of each product to use and the proper strength or dilution that is safe for use. Test results for using new products by applying to an area that is not going to show, and use with care. Use safety and protective gear properly, including gloves, protective eyewear, and respiratory protection.

Know which areas you are responsible for maintaining:

- Pantry appliances—blenders, juice machines, coffee equipment
- Refrigeration—ice machines, wine coolers, refrigerators
- Cleaning equipment-vacuums, steamers, carpet cleaning equip
- What filters and ventilation you are in charge of? A/C filters, dryers and lint removal
- Electronics and electrical equipment

Create a System for Inventories and Purchasing:

- Inventories and checklists of cleaning products
- Purchases
- Organization & reorganization
- Stowing items
- Organizing and re-organizing lockers, cupboards, and cabinets

Cleaning & Sanitation

Recently a friend of mine, who works on a sport fish boat, was infected by the potentially deadly staph infection MRSA. He is okay now, but it made me think about how up close and personal we all are, the kind of toxins and germs we are regularly exposed to, and how seriously ill one can get in a very short period of time. We come in contact with germs and bacteria on a regular basis, and a boat is the perfect environment for them to grow. So how do we keep germs under control?

This is an important topic as part of the general subject of hygiene and food safety. It is startling to learn how little some individuals know about the basics of good hygiene. Many of us have worked in restaurants and hotels and are aware of the standards that have to be upheld, but many people in the yachting industry are not. Here is a basic primer for two common areas: the bathroom and the galley/crew mess areas.

The Bathroom

There are lots of germs here and lots of opportunities to spread infection and disease. As a general rule, the best way to prevent germs from invading your body is to wash your hands often for 15-20 seconds each time. Soap and water don't actually kill germs; they lift them off and flush them away. As for antibacterial soaps, studies show that they are no better than regular soaps at reducing bacteria on hands, and, in fact, they have been shown to promote bacterial resistance.

Clean and disinfect the faucets and taps daily, because they are one of the most likely places to harbor superbugs like MRSA and other bacteria. Hand towels should be changed as often as possible, and paper towels may be a better option in high-traffic bathrooms Change your bath towels regularly, at least every three days, because damp towels can harbor *e coli* bacteria from our bodies and from droplets of spray from the toilet.

Every time you flush the toilet, some of the dirty water sprays into the air. Close the lid before flushing to prevent this kind of contamination. Closing the lid before flushing can also help end one of the most common conflicts that men encounter—putting the seat down after using the toilet...perhaps this could save your relationships as well as your health!!

Alene Keenan on bathroom duty
[Image courtesy of 123rf.com] | [Image courtesy of ezeliving.com]

The Galley/Crew Mess Areas

While bathrooms have a bad reputation for hosting threatening germs, most of the germs in a living area are actually located in the kitchen. The galley and crew mess are areas where germs such as salmonella, e coli, and even listeria can run rampant. No matter how often you clean, scrub, and wipe down food preparation areas, germs are always present. Food itself carries viruses, fungi, and protozoa, and the presence of these can lead to colds, flu, skin lesions, ciguatera, and various forms of food poisoning. Staph infections, including MRSA, live on skin and in the nose, so proper personal hygiene is crucial.

Studies have shown that sinks, towels, sponges, and cutting boards carry the most germs. Sponges and towels in particular are porous, wet, and full of spaces for germs to gather.

To cut down on contaminants, always use separate sponges for dishes and counters, and run them through the dishwasher frequently to kill germs. Microwaving them on high for one minute will also work. Disinfectant wipes or paper towels are a good option for countertops, since the contaminants go right into the trash each time. Take care when using wipes, because they are good at removing bacteria, but not killing it. Using it on a second surface just spreads germs around.

Cutting boards and counters have to be used and cleaned carefully to avoid cross-contamination. It is a good idea to use one cutting board for raw meats and poultry and another for produce.

[Image courtesy of sunseeker.com]

So what about hand sanitizer and hand wipes? Alcohol-based sanitizing gel kills 99% of germs on contact, making them a sure winner. For maximum effectiveness, apply to the palm of one hand and rub hands together, covering all surfaces, until they are dry. Most hand wipes and towelettes are less effective than hand sanitizers, but those highly saturated with 69.5% ethanol work really well.

Last but not least, you may be asked to use alcohol as a solvent to clean certain items and surfaces. There are two kinds that you will encounter, rubbing alcohol and denatured alcohol. Use both with extreme care, and neither is fit to drink. What is the difference between rubbing alcohol and denatured alcohol? According to research from the Proctor and Gamble website, denatured alcohol is ethanol to which toxic chemicals have been added, including methanol, gasoline, or isopropanol and it is not safe for use on the skin. Rubbing alcohol is another form of denatured alcohol, but it is safe to use on the skin. It promotes a cooling effect and is used as an antibacterial. Rubbing alcohol works great for sanitizing on stainless steel faucets and surfaces, glass, electronics, and cell phones, but vodka is just as effective and actually safer to use.

Working with Chlorine Bleach

Never mix chlorine bleach or any product containing chlorine bleach with ammonia or acidic products. This is a potentially dangerous combination. Store chlorinated products or any other dangerous products in their original containers and do not remove product labels. Dispose of empty cleaning supply containers; do not reuse them by filling with another product. Keep cleaning products away from food; and keep cleaning products away from children and pets.

Cleaning with No Guests Onboard

When no guests are present, the detailed cleaning and maintenance takes place. Various tools are used to make sure every surface, crevice, and crack is scrupulously clean. Break out the cotton buds, toothpicks, buckets, brushes, sponges and magic erasers! In yachting, your work is not finished until you have washed, dried, polished, buffed and "tooth-picked" in every room. It can take hours to clean and polish a single room properly!

Carpets and floors must be protected by runners custom-fitted to each room. Protect interior surfaces from ultraviolet light damage by keeping the blinds closed and the draperies drawn. Protect and maintain all crew areas, including individual crew cabins. Protect and maintain all refrigerators, vacuum cleaners, steam cleaners, air conditioning vents, air handlers, and any tools required to do your job.

Cleaning and Detailing

- Always protect the areas where you are cleaning
- Have all of the proper materials on hand when you begin
- Differentiate between levels of cleaning: daily and detail cleaning. Detail cleaning is cleaning with great care, using tools to clean, polish, wax, and buff surfaces
- When using spray bottles, apply cleaning supplies directly onto cleaning cloths, not onto the surface you are cleaning to avoid damaging other surfaces in the vicinity
- Aerosol sprays have a propellant that is unhealthy

Know Your Finishes

- Glass and windows (know what materials are they made of and what supplies are safe
- Different wood finishes:
    - Varnish: gloss or satin
    - Polished or waxed surfaces
    - Oiled surfaces
    - Painted or lacquered
    - Veneers: the surface is actually a very thin layer glued on
- Marble and stone
    - No strong cleaning products. Use pH neutral soap for washing
    - No acidic or abrasive cleaners
- Metals (not all metals are meant to be polished)
    - Know whether it is lacquered or coated
    - Know what type of metal is it: plated or solid
    - Stainless steel fixtures and fittings: brushed or polished

Preparing for Guests to Come Aboard

There is a certain kind of joy that you experience in getting the yacht ready for guests to come aboard. If you have completed a long passage, the boat will be practically disassembled, with everything wrapped and stowed to prevent breakage. When you arrive at your destination, everything gets put back together and you set the scene for a new season!

Lots of things can happen underway, so every area must be checked for damage or leakage; deck items stowed inside have to go back outside; stripped down rooms are reassembled; and every area is cleaned. Detail clean all areas and walls from the ceiling down to the floor. Remove and vacuum all sofa and chair cushions. Rotate the cushions as needed to insure even wear. Remove runners and vacuum and clean all floors. Clean all air-conditioning vents. Clean windows, mirrors, and any reflective surfaces. Any metal artwork, furniture, or brightwork that needs polishing should be taken care of. Wipe clean all the door handles. Clean the inside of all cabinets and drawers. Make all beds with fresh linens, including the mattress pads and pillow covers. Clean all heads and showers until they are spotless. As a final touch, fresh flowers, magazines, and information about local features and attractions are put on display for the guests to enjoy.

This is when teamwork and camaraderie come into play, with everyone working against the clock to get their jobs completed. Then, hopefully there's time for everyone to go out together and celebrate a successful journey and a successful transition to the next chapter. After that, it's time get ready to meet the demands of the job that lies ahead.

Cleaning when guests are onboard

Depending on the size of the boat and the number of crew, stews may rotate the service and housekeeping duties. This means that one stew will probably be responsible for housekeeping duties for the entire day, another may be in charge of laundry, while other stews are responsible for service set up and delivery. The stew(s) are responsible for dusting, vacuuming, and maintaining the cleanliness of the entire interior. Cabins must be detailed, beds made, and laundry started. Surfaces must be continually checked for fingerprints, including walls, windows, mirrors, countertops, tables and all heads. Magazines and personal items must be continually straightened and organized throughout the day. Pillows and cushions must be fluffed as needed. Heads must be checked and detailed on a regular basis. Laundry and ironing must be continually kept going, so that all laundry is completed and returned by the end of the day. Staff should try to be as discrete as possible. If a guest enters a room while you are cleaning, quietly pick up your supplies and leave the room until they have gone.

[Image courtesy of howardproducts.com]

Checklist of Additional Housekeeping Items

All linens and towels for the staterooms and heads must be fresh and ready for use, and be sure fresh robes and slippers are available for guests. Use the following checklist to ensure that you have covered all of the bases before your guests step aboard.

- Supply all heads with fresh towels and mats.
- Restock all toiletries and paper products.
- Restock supplies of stationery, pens, etc.
- Check batteries in all remote controls for television, DVD players, lights, fans, etc.
- Check to see that all electronic equipment is charged and working.

- Double-check that all light bulbs are functional.
- Restock stew pantries and cleaning cabinets.
- Stock bar and wine coolers.
- Double check that all requests from preference list have been obtained.
- Be sure the pilothouse is detailed. Use caution when cleaning any electronic equipment. Note that cans of compressed air are good for cleaning delicate items.
- Clean all appliances (laundry machines, irons, roller presses, refrigerators, microwaves, ice machines, etc.).
- Be sure all appliances in the galley are clean and polished (coffee machines, cappuccino machines, toasters, etc.).
- Fluff and buff every area of the boat. Set out floral arrangements, candies, magazines, and brochures that highlight local attractions.
- Walk through one last time and make sure everything is spotless!
- Prepare "welcome cocktails" and invite your guests aboard!

Checklist for recommended cleaning supplies

You don't want to be caught out at sea without all of the tools necessary to maintain a 5-star service. Use the following as your starter checklist for cleaning supplies:

- One or more canister-style vacuum cleaner with attachments
- Carpet sweeper
- Dust pan and brush
- Floor mop or wet floor cleaner
- Blind duster, feather duster, lamb's wool duster
- Small paint brushes for dusting small areas and getting into corners
- Canned compressed air
- Variety of cleaning cloths – microfiber and cotton
- Rubber gloves
- Antiseptic wipes
- Garbage bags in various sizes
- Cleaning brushes including toothbrushes
- Sponges
- Cotton swabs
- Paper towels
- Mild dishwashing liquid

- Automatic dishwashing liquid
- Silver polish
- Marble/stone polish
- Wood cleaner and polish
- General purpose liquid cleaner
- Rubbing alcohol
- Hydrogen peroxide
- Distilled white vinegar
- Air freshener
- Disinfectant spray
- Carpet spot cleaners
- Baking soda
- Ammonia
- Club soda
- Salt
- Glass surface cleaner
- Citrus based cleaner
- Leather cleaner and conditioner
- Bleach
- Laundry detergent
- Fabric softener
- Nail polish remover
- Various stain removers
- OxyClean
- Various laundry treatment supplies
- Spray starch if used
- Cleaning products for irons
- Iron(s)
- Ironing board

[Image courtesy of www.doityourself.com]

Laundry

"Sometimes I feel like throwing in the towel. But you know what that means...more laundry!" —Anonymous

Clothing is another expensive possession that you will be responsible for on yachts. There is a lot to know about clothing construction and care, for both crew uniforms and guest clothing. Inexperienced stews should not be handed the responsibility of dealing with expensive clothing. Learning how to do laundry is a detailed process, and stews have to start at the very beginning. One of my favorite basic-level books about laundry is *Betty's Book of Laundry Secrets* by Betty Faust and Maria Rodale. It is simple, but gives a thorough overview. Another terrific guide that is a bit irreverent and somewhat amusing is *Field Guide to Stains* by Virginia M. Friedman. Sometimes when you are buried under a mountain of laundry you need to see the lighter side of things and maybe you could use a good laugh! To delve deeper and uncover the science behind the cleaning and clothing industries, Cheryl Mendelson has written two books: *Home Comforts* and *Laundry: The Home Comforts Book of Caring for Clothes and Linens*.

Steve Boorstein, aka "The Clothing Doctor" has written *The Ultimate Guide to Shopping and Caring for Clothing: Everything you need to know...from blue jeans to ball gowns!* This book will educate you and empower you. Use it as a reference guide for issues with fabrics and their proper care. It is fascinating and you may catch yourself reading it cover to cover just for enjoyment. Steve Boorstein is a graduate of the International Fabricare Institute and he has conducted seminars for Chanel Boutique, Saks Fifth Avenue, Neiman Marcus, and Nordstrom's department stores in the United States. He also provides guidelines for drapery and upholstery care.

Laundry Overview

Handling guest and crew laundry is an important, never-ending, technically difficult part of a stew's job that requires a lot of knowledge and skill. Always check the manufacturer's care tags and follow the directions. Some items require dry cleaning, so they must be sent out, or else refused if the yacht is located where there are no dry cleaning services. Do not accept any guest items for laundry that you feel could create problems.

[Image courtesy of 1800sailaway.com]

Guest sheets, towels, and table linens will be laundered separately and on their own schedule; they will require more time and care than crew linens. When there are no guests onboard, the quantity of laundry is substantially less; it is the crew laundry that makes up the majority of the laundry workload.

Each crew member may be responsible for his or her own personal items and the machines will be made available to them when there are no guests onboard. Crew sheets, towels and uniforms will generally be done by the stews during the day, and a schedule for laundering crew bed linens should be set up.

Front-loading vs. top-loading machines:

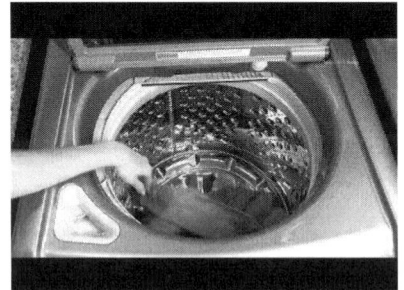

[Images courtesy of article.wn.com]

    At the very least, you must know how to sort laundry. One single load of laundry that is incorrectly sorted can cause hundreds of dollars' worth of damage to high-priced clothing, or any clothing, for that matter.

[Image courtesy of teacherspayteachers.com]

Be sure to separate:

- Dark fabrics from light and white fabrics
- Heavily soiled clothing (engineer's coveralls, galley towels and aprons) from lightly soiled and delicate clothing. Remember that items from the galley need to be treated to kill bacteria.
- Fabrics by washing temperature and care instructions
- Any delicate items that need to be in a mesh laundry bag
- Any fabrics that will leave lint on other items, such as towels. Microfiber cleaning cloths should be laundered separately from terrycloth, or they will be ruined
- Colors that bleed should always be separated: reds, purples, anything you know will fade onto other clothing. Use Color Catcher sheets religiously.

Before putting clothes into the laundry machine, always button buttons, hook bras, and zip up zippers before you wash items. It will prevent damage to fabrics and retain clothing shape.

Also, be sure to check clothing for spots and pretreat with a special presoak solution. Soak stubborn spots overnight. In dry cleaning parlance, a spot is removable; a stain is not. Be very cautious when you use bleach on or around clothing. It is very easy to ruin something accidentally when you are using chlorine bleach. Make sure that all surfaces are free of bleach residue after use. There are color-safe bleaches for colored items, and hydrogen peroxide applied sparingly works wonders on white fabrics that have bloodstains. Check treated areas when you take them out of the machine. If the spot did not come out, do not dry the item in the dryer. It will set the stain. Instead, try another stain removal tactic.

Fabric Care

Natural fibers, such as linen and cotton, are the most frequently chosen fabrics for table and bed linens, and you must know the basics about how to care for them.

Cotton has a number of properties that make it an ideal choice for table and bed linens. It is extremely versatile in weight, texture, and construction; it is strong when wet, not prone to pulling or seam slippage, and the fibers are absorbent. Cotton draws heat away from the body and is free from static electricity. However, there are several cautionary notes about cotton to be aware of. It can deteriorate if mildewed, and it may be weakened by excessive exposure to sunlight. Cotton has a tendency to wrinkle unless it is treated with a special finish; and it may also shrink quite a lot in hot water or in a dryer.

Pre-shrunk cotton can be washed in hot water as long as it is color safe. Chlorine bleach may turn white cottons yellow. Fabric softener will reduce wrinkling, but note that it is not good to use on towels because it will make them less absorbent. Tumble dry cotton on medium heat but do not over-dry. Press cotton with a hot iron while still damp until it is completely dry, or use a steam iron with a slightly dampened press cloth.

Linen is beautiful, durable, elegant, and it has a natural luster. It can be made into sheer, medium, or heavyweight fabrics. Linen does not attract lint, but it does have a tendency to wrinkle. It is exceptionally strong, but stiff. Linen may show wear at the edges and folds over time and it has a poor affinity for dyes so bright colors and black may be unstable. Linen fabric will easily shrink and it will deteriorate from mildew.

Wash linen at the medium temperature setting in warm water. Be cautious with chlorine bleach because it may weaken the fibers. Linen launders well if it has been pre-shrunk. Tumble dry linen on a regular heat setting, but remove it when it is still very damp. Iron linen on a high heat setting. To preserve durability, creases should not be pressed into folds.

Laundry with Guests Onboard

Guest laundry provides enough work for one stew to be dedicated to doing only laundry all day long. It is a continuous, ongoing task and it is important to keep moving the laundry through so it can be finished every day. You may be surprised at the types of clothing you will be asked to launder and press. It is not uncommon to be asked to care for clothing that costs in the hundreds, if not the thousands, of dollars. Relax, take a deep breath, and approach this reasonably. If you have any questions or concerns, ask the chief stew or the guest who has given you the article of clothing for guidance. It is better to get clarification on how to proceed than to take the chance of ruining any article of clothing. It helps to have an iron that provides lots of steam!

Keep a stain removal guide on hand, and learn the international laundry symbols for choosing temperatures for washing, drying and ironing clothing. For a downloadable copy of common laundering and dry cleaning symbols, go to www.textileaffairs.com

Sorting laundry is the first, very important step. The categories for sorting laundry and ironing include:

- Crew uniforms, sheets, and towels
- Galley towels and aprons
- All breakfast, lunch, and dinner table linens
- Guest bed linens and towels
- Guest clothing and personal items, which often require hand washing. Note fabric content, color fastness, and care instructions

Log and tag all guest items taken for laundering to keep track of which cabin they are from so they can be returned properly. Inspect each item for spots and use the proper stain removal technique as needed. Most of the guests' clothing and personal items will be ironed, often including socks and underwear, unless the care instructions say otherwise, or if it is a delicate item subject to damage. All guest clothing and personal items should be properly folded.

If there is no housekeeping guide already written for the yacht, you need to create one. For inspiration and ideas, Martha Stewart's *Homekeeping Handbook* is an excellent resource for general tips on laundry, ironing, folding and storing bed linens, towels and table linens.

Ironing

As a yacht stewardess, you are expected to know how to iron. You will spend hours ironing every day when you are on laundry duty. If you know how to sew, you have a definite advantage because you have learned how to iron as you go when you construct garments. Following are some general hints for ironing:

- Fabrics will be smoother if they are ironed while they are damp, so remove them from the dryer before they are fully dry. Smooth out seams and pleats on garments and pull linens back into shape immediately.

- If you let items dry fully in the dryer, dampen them with water from a spray mist bottle before ironing with a steam iron. Check the manufacturer's directions for your iron to determine whether or not you should use distilled water in the iron; using distilled water is no longer the standard practice.

- If you are using spray sizing or starch, spray each item and then allow the product to soak into the piece for a few moments. This will prevent excessive product build-up on the sole-plate of the iron, and save you the trouble of having to remove the unattractive product that comes jetting out of the steam vents and soils your freshly laundered clothing.

- Sort your ironing so the lower temperature items are done first, such as synthetics and silks. As the iron heats up, work on heavier fabrics as you go – woolens, cottons, and linens.

Ironing lace, silk, and wool: For these items, use a pressing cloth or iron inside out. Do not slide the iron back and forth; lift and lower it.

Ironing metallic, beaded or sequined fabric: Place on a soft surface such as a towel and press gently using a low heat setting.

Ironing shirts and jackets: Start at the point of the collar, working toward the center. Iron the yoke by arranging one shoulder over the end of the ironing board, then do the same for the other shoulder. Do the sleeves next, working down from the underarm; a sleeve board is very helpful. Next, open the cuffs and iron them flat. Then iron the back of the shirt, slipping it over the wide-end of the board and shifting as needed. Finally, iron the two halves of the front, or if it doesn't open, slip it over the board and finish.

Ironing pants: If the pants have cuffs, unfold them and brush out any loose material. Turn the waistband inside out and pull out the pockets to iron them flat. Iron the zipper placket. On the right side of garment, iron the waistband and the rest of the top; and then repeat this process on the left side. Put the leg seams together in the middle and fold pants the long way. Lay them flat on the board, and then fold back the top leg. Iron the inside of the lower leg, then turn and iron the outside. Repeat this process with the other leg. Lastly, iron all four thicknesses of the two legs together.

Ironing skirts: Iron from the hem to the waist in long strokes, but lift and lower the iron when pressing gathers. For pleats, arrange pleats on the ironing board and pin or hold them in place. Iron from the top to the bottom but not over the pins.

Ironing dresses: Iron the lining first. Continue to the top of the dress as if you were ironing a blouse. A dress that doesn't open should be pulled over the board; then iron front and back. Lift and press underneath any collar, then press the collar itself. Some dresses may require steaming only.

General Ironing Notes

Be sure the sole plate of the iron and the ironing board cover are clean of any starch buildup that could transfer to fabrics. Always set to the proper temperature for the fabric, and use a slightly dampened cloth to protect the surface of suits, corduroys, or wool sweaters. Clothes should be aired after ironing to be sure they are totally dry from the steam before they are put away.

Suits or jackets do not usually crease except inside the elbows. Cover the wrinkled area with a damp cloth and press. Steam, rather than iron, a jacket lining. Suits and suit trousers should be steamed, not pressed.

Brushing Clothing

One of the most important parts of clothing care is examining for stains and deciding whether or not to launder or dry clean the item. Many items are not meant to be washed, and would need to be dry-cleaned. To cut down on the amount of visits to the dry cleaner's, brushing is a way to maintain clothing in between visits. Brushing refreshes clothes and removes dust and food particles. It also relaxes fabric fibers and removes wrinkles. It is the best way to keep suits clean and it improves the appearance of most clothing.

Use a natural bristle brush and brush clothes each time they are worn. Brush one section of a garment at a time, using a firm, brushing motion going against the nap and then back down. Use a lint brush for hair or any particles that cling.

Brushing velvet: Use another piece of velvet to rub the velvet down the nap of the garment.

Brushing tweeds and wools: Tweeds and wools should be brushed each time they are worn.

Brushing jackets: Always empty the pockets so they can lie flat. Turn up the collar and lapels and lay the jacket flat, face downward. Brush the nap up first, then down.

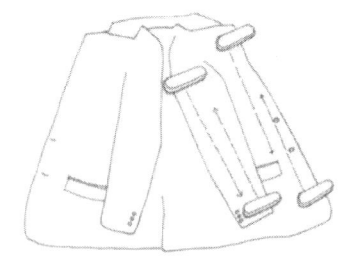

[Image courtesy of the butlerscloset.com and theartofmanliness.com]

Mending Clothing

Ensure that you have onboard the variety of materials you need for sewing on buttons and mending clothing for both owner/guests and crew. There are some great videos online at www.ehow.com that give detailed instructions on how to properly mend clothing.

Sewing buttons: Use heavy thread for sewing buttons onto jackets and coats. Thread the needle and make a small knot at the end. Begin stitching from the front side so that the knot is under the button. Stitch up from the back, using the same stitching pattern that was used on the existing buttons. Do not pull stitches tight; leave about 1/8 inch of thread between the cloth and the button to avoid puckering. Crisscross the thread at least 6 times on a 4-hole button. Wrap the thread 3 or 4 times around the shank (the thread between the cloth and the button). Finish off with 2 tiny stitches through the back. Pull the thread behind the button on the right side. Make a knot and trim off the ends.

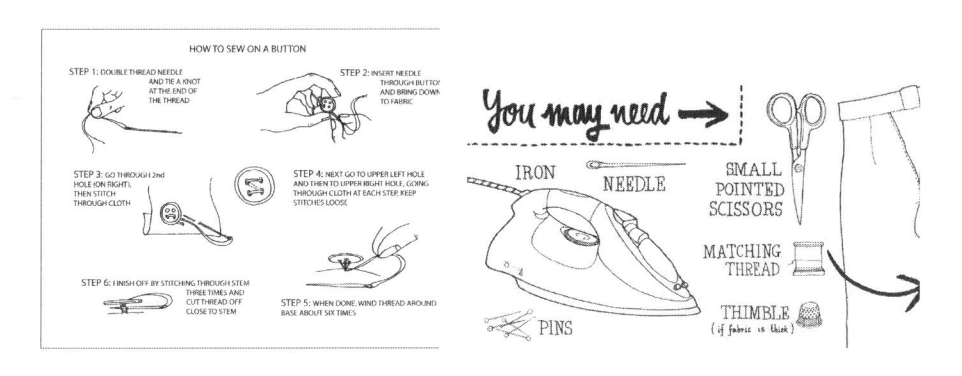

[Image courtesy of collegetimes.com and theguardian.com]

Mending a ripped seam: Turn the garment inside out and iron seam out flat so that the edges meet and the line of the stitching is clear. Using the line of undamaged stitches as your guide, line the fabric edges up and secure by pinning them with straight pins. Pins should be at right angles to the fabric edges. Knot the thread before you begin. Start sewing an inch above where the seams came apart. Follow the line of the stitch marks and finish an inch below the end of the opening. Complete with a knot.

Keeping the Laundry Room Clean & Sanitized

Once a month, disinfect the washers by running a load on hot with bleach, because it is toxic to bacteria. It is important to use the proper dilutions of bleach, or it is not effective. More is not necessarily better because it wears out the rubber parts of the machine.

To avoid cross-contamination, always wash food-related items, such as dishcloths and kitchen towels separately and in hot water. Separate galley towels from stew towels, since this reduces the chances for cross-contamination. And please, please, please, rinse food debris from the galley towels before giving them to stews to launder!!! The galley towels often harbor grease and oil, and food-borne bacteria can cling to it. Not only can it make an unsightly mess or our clean dishes and glasses, it is unsanitary. Wash galley and stew towels in hot water, occasionally run a load of bleach with them, and dry completely.

Guests and crew are given laundry bags for their uniforms and personal clothing. When they are brought in for the stews to wash, it is tempting to overload the machine in order to save time and space – but don't do that. Wash bathroom towels, sweaty workout gear, and underwear in hot water, separate from uniforms and other clothing items. Do not over-stuff the machines, because the water has to be able to circulate freely to remove and flush away germs and bacteria as well as dirt.

Temperature is important, too, for safety as well as for fabric care instructions. Washing in cold or lukewarm water removes only about 80 percent of bacteria. This is important to note because germs can be spread through the entire load and can remain on the walls of the washer. To be safe, wash high-risk items on hot and dry completely.

Plumbing and Engineering: What You Need to Know

Although it usually falls to the engineering department to maintain the septic systems on the boat, it is helpful to have a little knowledge of what is happening below-decks. The toilet systems vary from boat to boat, and it is vital that you know what products, if any, are safe to use.

One thing, however, is the same on every boat: the system is delicate, and the most important rule is that with the exception of toilet tissue, nothing should go into the toilet that has not first gone through the body. Keep in mind that none of those so-called "flushable wipes" are safe to dispose of in the septic system, and be sure the guests are aware of this.

Your department head, captain or engineer will provide you with the basic maintenance information you need to be responsible for. Make sure you follow the rules meticulously. If there is ever a problem with the head system, report it immediately, because the situation can rapidly deteriorate – and that is a most unpleasant experience for everyone involved.

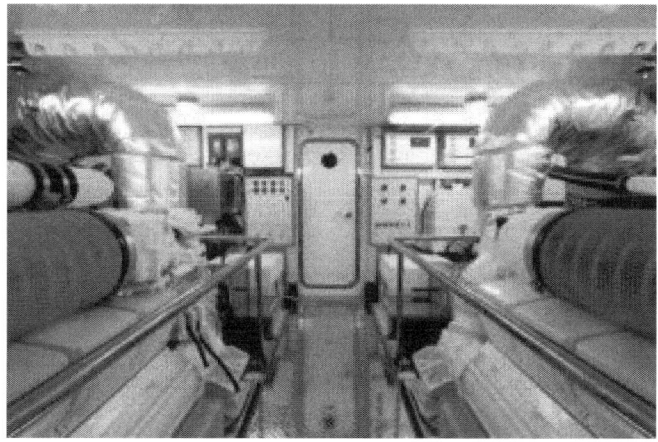

[Image courtesy of cruisejobfinder.com and navitrol.com]

Chapter 10

Flowers & Flower Arrangement Basics

"With freedom, books, flowers and the moon, who could not be happy?" —Oscar Wilde

One of the best ways to brighten a room is with a beautiful display of fresh flowers. Part of your job as a yacht stew will include floral arrangement and maintenance. At the beginning of your career, you may feel overwhelmed at the thought of creating arrangements for different locations throughout the boat, but with practice your skills will improve.

[Image courtesy of ezliving.com]

As a first step, you will need to know the number of arrangements you will need, where they go, the dimensions of each arrangement space, what style of arrangement you want, and the colors and flowers you want to use. You will need this information whether you order flower arrangements from a floral shop or you buy fresh flowers and arrange them yourself.

The yacht will probably have a selection of vases chosen by the owner or the decorator on board. There may be strict guidelines about the types of flowers and the arrangement styles allowable for these vases, as well as specific placement rules for the finished arrangements. Photos of examples of arrangements from each area are very helpful. The dining room centerpiece arrangement dimensions will vary according to the size of the room and of the table. The centerpiece for the table should be below the line of sight, and in proportion to the space available as determined by how much china, glassware, and cutlery is used in table setting. An arrangement that is too large may crowd the dining space.

Sometimes the particular flowers you request will not be available. There may not be very many types of flowers to choose from, but as you gain experience, you will learn to work with whatever is accessible. You should always have floral tools on hand, including floral tape, flower food, flower foam, and pruning shears and clippers, at the very least.

There are some terrific books about flower arranging to learn from. One of my favorites is *The Flower Arranging Expert* by Dr. D. G. Hessayon. It's very old-school but it breaks down the components very well. He goes into great detail about the basic mechanical items and equipment needed for flower arranging. Mechanical items include different kinds of floral foam, clay, waterproof adhesive tape, pinholders, frogs, and other items that keep the foliage in place inside a container. Equipment includes scissors, knives, wire, paper floral tape for wrapping stems, buckets, misters, and watering cans. The book has information and instruction about floral materials. It also includes detailed introductory guidelines for arrangement designs and styles.

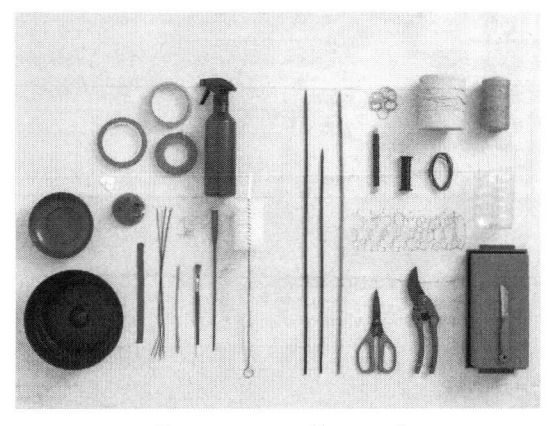

[Image courtesy of hgtv.com]

Other wonderful books include all of Paula Pryke's books, but especially *Flowers: The Complete Book of Floral Design* and *Flower School: Mastering the Art of Floral Design*. Michael Gaffney's *Design Star: Lessons from the New York School of Flower Design* is another fantastic reference.

Floral art in Europe is much older than here in America. Japanese Ikebana is much older still, and dates back over 1000 years. There are many books on Ikebana, but one of my favorites is a book by Shozo Sato called *Ikebana: Create Beautiful Flower Arrangements with this Traditional Japanese Art*.

In any event, flowers are a big part of creating an elegant ambiance on a yacht, and they represent a considerable investment of time and money. It is really important to learn as much as you can about them and know how to maintain them properly to make them last as long as possible. Flower arranging is an artistic skill that requires considerable hands-on practice.

Conditioning & Prepping Flowers

If you are arranging flowers yourself, you must condition them to strengthen them and add vitality as soon as possible. When flowers are brought onboard, the stems are already cut and left exposed to air. The cut will begin to heal and seal itself off, and then no water can get into the stem. To condition them, recut the stems at a 45-degree angle and place them in water. The angle keeps the stems from sitting flat on the bottom of the vase and it creates a greater surface area for the stem to absorb water. If you have time, let them drink for a while.

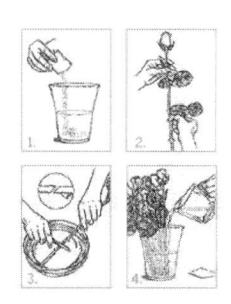

[Image courtesy of marthastewart.com]

Cut flowers need sugar for food and something acidic to help them absorb water. The little packet of floral food that comes with fresh cut flowers will provide all that they need. If you don't have that available, here is Martha Stewart's recipe to make your own:

> **Cut Flower Food:** For every quart of water, add two aspirins or the juice of half a lemon, 1 teaspoon of sugar, and a few drops of chlorine bleach to kill bacteria.

Before you start putting an arrangement together, be sure that the vases you are using are clean and free of bacteria and then fill them with tepid water. Next, take the flowers and remove any leaves that sit under the waterline. This helps keep algae and bacteria from growing and helps your flowers to last longer. Keeping them in a cool area also prolongs their life.

In the vase, the stems should always be covered, so check the water level daily. Sometimes the water will get cloudy, so you may have to pour it out and make sure it has no bacteria. Be sure to check the stems at least once every two or three days, and recut them so they can absorb water.

Designing the Arrangement

When you start to design your arrangement, you need to think about the artistic line you are creating, the flowers you are using, and the way the different materials will look together.

Examples of the components of a flower arrangement:

- *Line materials* are the first elements placed in a floral design, determining the height and width of the arrangement. If no line materials are used in the arrangement, the flowers themselves determine the line.
- *Dominant materials* are placed after the line materials. Usually these are *form* flowers like lilies and anthurium and *mass* flowers like roses. They are inserted within the form established by the line materials.

- *Secondary materials* will usually consist of smaller *mass* flowers, spaced symmetrically between the dominant materials throughout the design.
- *Filler materials* "fill in" open spaces throughout the design, but are not mandatory.
- *Special materials* are added to create visual texture. This could include moss, vines, or fruit.
- *Accent materials* are also an important consideration in a floral design. This is the use of objects such as a figurine to act as focal point of the composition, or simply using color as the focal point.

The mass and form flowers themselves can be used in the same way as line materials. Use them to establish the top and outer boundaries and concentrate on symmetry in the design.

Types of Flowers

Line flowers

Line flowers are tall, thin, and linear. They include the Bells of Ireland, gladiolus, snapdragon, delphinium, ginger, and liatrus.

Mass flowers

Mass flowers are secondary materials in a floral design. They are named for the mass or bulk they contribute to the arrangement. The majority of round flowers are classified as mass flowers. They include hydrangeas, roses, peonies, dahlias, and daisies.

Form flowers

Form flowers are named for their unique shape and form. They are used as dominant material in floral design. Form flowers include lilies, anthurium, bird of paradise, iris, and the Star of Bethlehem.

Filler flowers

Filler flowers are used to fill in the areas between the major floral elements. They include baby's breath, statice, and solidaster.

Vases

Most vases are a variation on one of the following five shapes:

- Bottle – narrow at top
- Sphere – creates a lush globe when filled
- Pail – widens at top, giving flowers freedom
- Cylinder – best for showing off big bunches of flowers
- Low pan – good for floating blooms or stems anchored with frogs It is the only shape that does not control the stems

[Images courtesy of vasekino.net] [Image courtesy of houzz.com]
[Image courtesy of homedit.com] [Image courtesy of vasekino.net]
[Image courtesy of deluxehire.co.uk]

Chapter 11

Getting Hired

"What would life be if we had no courage to attempt anything?" —Vincent van Gogh

If you would like to pursue a career in yachting, be prepared to work hard, physically and emotionally; to be a team player; to have a flexible attitude; and to be willing to go above and beyond the call of duty whenever it is necessary, at any hour of the day or night. The yachting lifestyle can be challenging, but the rewards can be amazing. You will travel to many different places, learn a lot of cool stuff, and have wonderful opportunities for down time in some pretty incredible places. You will have experiences that other people can only dream about. The lifestyle is intense, and creates a special kind of camaraderie and an awesome sense of accomplishment. It can be immensely gratifying to bond together as a team in a high-pressure situation, and create a magical experience for the yacht owners and their guests.

Just as in any other industry, the more experience you have, the easier it is to find work within that field. It is a double bind situation: it can seem impossible to get a job without some experience, and at the same time, it is impossible to get experience without a job. The minimum requirements that you will need to have are your STCW certification and ENG 1 medical certificate. It helps to have background knowledge and skill in waitressing, wine service, bartending, and other hotel and food service areas.

There are two books on the subject of jobs in the super yacht industry that I highly recommend. Both of them have a vast amount of detail about the industry. The first one, *The Insider's Guide to Becoming a Yacht Stewardess:*

Confessions From My Years Afloat With the Rich and Famous by Julie Perry, is part memoir and part how-to for getting a job in the yachting industry. It is full of pertinent information and personal anecdotes. The second book, *Working On Yachts and Superyachts* by Jennifer Errico, is chock-full of details that you need to know about working on super yachts.

Go Where the Jobs Are

If you're about to go job hunting, location is critical. It can be tough to get that first break into the yachting world. You have to go where the jobs are. It is far easier to get started in the Interior Crew industry if you are located in one of the busiest cities for private yachting, and there are only a few cities that qualify as the best locations in the world for this type of employment. Your best chances for employment are in:

- Antibes, France
- Palma de Mallorca, Spain
- Fort Lauderdale, Florida
- Newport, Rhode Island
- St. Thomas, US Virgin Islands
- St. Martin/St. Maarten, West Indies
- Antigua, West Indies

The yachting industry follows the Earth's seasons, so some ports are busier and therefore better at certain times than others. Each season lasts 4 or 5 months, and the remainder of the year is usually scheduled for shipyard maintenance periods. The summer Med Season typically starts in April or May, with Antibes, France and Palma de Mallorca, Spain being the hot spots for hiring in Europe. At about the same time, yachts in the United States will be preparing for the New England, Bahamas, or West Coast/Alaska season. Fort Lauderdale, Florida and Newport, Rhode Island are good cities to look for yacht jobs on the East Coast, and San Diego is a good place to be on the West Coast for the summer months. In September, the boats will be moving into position for the winter season. Many will be heading to the Fort Lauderdale International Boat Show, held in October every year; or the Antigua boat show in December. Then the Caribbean winter season begins.

Before you pack everything and head off to one of these key destinations, be sure to do your homework. Learn where you will need a visa and/or passport, and if so, what type. Learn the areas of each town where the yachting industry is concentrated, and determine in advance what mode of transportation you will use to get around. Look on the Internet to determine where you might live in relation to the yacht industry areas and don't forget to investigate crew housing opportunities. Also, be sure to learn enough of the language to be able to function in that country.

It is important to have enough money with you to be able to live for several weeks or even months, until you get a job. Plan to live frugally, and don't get caught up in the social scene, or you will run out of money quickly. Try not to be discouraged. Keep in mind that just about everyone started at the bottom and worked their way up. Entry-level positions, part-time day working jobs, and even delivery crew positions are the best way to learn the ropes and start making contacts. Go to networking events to meet people in the industry. Get up early, walk the docks where you can, and try to get hired for your first position. If you don't find something right away, keep trying. People will see you out there and they will see your determination. Be enthusiastic, be professional, and make a good impression. Have lots of resumes and business cards to hand out. Talk to everybody and let them know you are looking for work. Many, many jobs are found simply by being in the right place at the right time and telling the right person that you are looking for a position.

Crew Employment Agencies

Crew agencies and yacht management/recruitment firms are a huge part of the yachting industry scene. Crew agencies do not hire you—they introduce you to the people who will hire you. Do not underestimate the value of forming professional relationships with crew agents. They are seasoned professionals who know how to sell your skills to potential employers who will also pick up the employment agency fees to hire you. Once again, you need to have your STCW requirements, some experience and references for them to be able to consider you as a candidate, but register with all of them and try to start building some sort of relationship with them. Crew agency personnel are extremely busy, and it can be difficult to get an interview until you have some experience under your belt. You may have a good chance to meet agents at networking events, and this could be a crucial first step in getting an opportunity to set up an interview.

Crew agents will work with you as you progress through your yachting career and can make your work progression rewarding and seamless. Be courteous and professional in relating to them. Thank them for their time in interviewing you, follow any advice they may give you about your appearance and resume/CV, and keep them informed about your availability so they don't spend time trying to place you if you have already found a position.

Trade Publications and Advertisements

The Internet also turns out to be one of the best sources to look for jobs in trade publications and other sources of online advertising. Most yachting industry trade publications have their own websites, which have an employment section with active listings. On the Internet you can also search for positions by title. The Triton, Dockwalk, and The Crew Report are great places to start. Most industry trade publications have classified ads placed by owners and captains who are looking for opportunities to keep the agency fees in their bank accounts. Be cautious, however, because Internet scams for yacht jobs exist, as they do in any industry. Use common sense and always think about your personal safety when meeting with anyone you have connected with online.

Dock Walking and Daywork

Dock walking, just as the name implies, is the term used to describe crew members who take their resume and business cards and head down to the area where the yachts are docked. Walking along the dock and approaching the gangway/passerelle, you ask if they are looking to hire a new stew. Dock walking has been a long-held tradition around docked ships for some time, but it is not as easy to do nowadays. It is illegal in many places today, for safety and security reason. It can also be an issue with immigration if your work permits and visa are not in order. If you are able to gain access legally to marinas and shipyards, try to make contact with people. Even if they say "no," try to hand them a business card because the next day or sometimes even an hour later their "no" will turn into a "yes" and you will be contacted. Actually, if you just relax and have fun with it, you will find yourself having a great time meeting other people employed in your industry and passing out your business cards.

Lastly, don't forget that there are long-term opportunities that can become available from the people who are testing out day workers. Sometimes there is a permanent position available, but the captain and chief stew want a chance to actually work with someone on a temporary basis to test them out. If it doesn't turn into an offer of permanent work, thank them and leave on the best terms possible. Ask the Captain for a reference. Your name may be the first one they think of when a permanent position comes up. Over time, your network of contacts in the yachting industry will grow, and it will become progressively easier to locate openings. The website, www.daywork123.com, in the United States lists jobs on a daily basis. Many yachting magazines and newspapers list jobs on their websites, especially those mentioned above: The Triton, Dockwalk, and The Crew Report.

Putting Your Best Self Forth

"Always put your best foot forward, but don't step on other people's toes." —Anonymous

The following are tips to increase the chances of finding a job. It is always a good idea to be open and friendly and to network at every opportunity. You never know when you might meet someone who can help you find your next position.

These suggestions are important for meeting people in general, but are especially so when you will be interacting with owners, brokers, captains, department heads and crew agents. They will quickly assess your level of professionalism by your appearance, poise and demeanor. Your work qualifications are of the utmost importance, but that first 15 seconds after you meet anyone sets the stage for whatever transpires next. Plan ahead and plan conservatively.

- Taking a conservative approach is the best way to go. Be aware that the less skin you show, the more power you have in life (and in an interview). Tattoos and piercings are still unacceptable in many instances and could actually keep you from being considered for a job, so remove excessive jewelry and cover up tattoos.

- Baring tank tops and sexy, low-cut T-shirts say way more about you than most professional people want to know, so wear clothing that covers more than it reveals. Remember that an opinion is formed about you within the first 15 seconds, and that opinion is not easily changed.

- Make an effort to become a great networker. Introduce yourself to everyone, carry lots of business cards, and have your resume handy in case someone asks for it. Don't hesitate to let people know what job you are looking for. Be clear, direct and honest about your skills.

- Crew agents will likely play an important part in your career development, and it's a good idea to register with several agencies. After your registration is complete, make an appointment to visit the offices in person. And do make an appointment; it is unprofessional and inconsiderate to just "pop in" unannounced. However, before setting an appointment, understand how crew agencies work, because they can be your biggest allies when you are looking for a job.

- Crew agencies help fill job openings. They introduce crew to prospective employers to be considered for placement. If the crew member is a good fit, she will be put forward to the employer, and the employer will decide whether to interview the candidate. And the employer will decide whether that crew member is right for the position. If a candidate is successfully placed, the agency collects a fee.

- Remember, the agency introduces crew to potential employers; it does not decide whether or not a crew member will be hired for a position.

Crew agents want to meet you to put a face to a name and to see if they can learn more about you. Show them the same courtesy you would show a prospective employer. Dress appropriately, cover any tattoos, and remove most of your jewelry, including all your piercings jewelry.

Employers are looking for diverse and specific attributes to fill open positions on their boats; and owners and department heads may have a certain profile in mind. And the vessel itself has a unique profile. All in all, everyone wants to ensure a good fit.

Keep in mind also that this is a unique industry that compares people not only on their skills and experience, but also on their appearance, age and general physical condition. What you need to do is put your best self forward in a positive, professional way.

In all fairness, there are some inappropriate employers out there as well, but that can be true in many industries.

Over the past few years, there have been big changes in the economy and within the yachting industry. But there will always be a place for confident, skilled professionals. Keep looking, keep learning, keep growing and keep offering your own special talents and skills to the world.

Appendix A
Resources and Recommended Reading

- *Roberts' Guide for Butlers and Other Household Staff* by Robert Roberts

- *Mrs. Beeton's Book of Household Management* by Isabella Beeton

- *Kiss, Bow, or Shake Hand* by Terri Morrison and Wayne Conway

- *Remarkable Service: A Guide to Winning and Keeping Customers* by The Culinary Institute of America

- *The Rituals of Dinner* by Margaret Visser

- *The Deluxe Food Lovers' Companion* by Sharon Tyler Herbst and Ron Herbst

- *The Art of the Table* by Suzanne Von Drachenfels

- *Tiffany's Table Manners for Teenagers* by Walter Hoving

- *Housekeeping* by Martha Stewart

- *Mrs. Starkey's Original Guide to Private Service* by Mrs. Mary Louise Starkey

- *Discovering Wine* by Joanna Simon

- Kevin Zraly's *Windows on the World Complete Wine Course*

- *How to Mix Drinks* by Professor Jerry Thomas

- *The Bon Vivant's Companion* by Professor Jerry Thomas

- *Drinks* by Vincent Gasnier

- *Professional Bartending* by Adam W. Freeth

- *Drinkology* by James Waller

- *The Art of the Cocktail Party* by Leslie Brenner

- *The London Ritz Book of Afternoon Tea*

- *Homekeeping Handbook* by Martha Stewart

- *Caring for Your Family Treasures* by Jane S. Long and Richard W. Long

- *Home Comforts: The Art and Science of Keeping House*, by Cheryl Mendelson

- *Betty's Book of Laundry Secrets* by Betty Faust and Maria Rodale

- *Field Guide to Stains* by Virginia M. Friedman

- *Laundry: The Home Comforts Book of Caring for Clothes and Linens* by Cheryl Mendelson

- *The Ultimate Guide to Shopping and Caring for Clothing* by Steve Boorstein

- *The Flower Arranging Expert* by Dr. D. G. Hessayon

- *The Complete Book of Floral Design* by by Paula Pryke

- *Flower School: Mastering the Art of Floral Design* by Paula Pryke

- *Design Star: Lessons from the New York School of Flower Design* by Michael Gaffney

- *Ikebana-Create Beautiful Flower Arrangements with this Traditional Japanese Art* by Shozo Sato

- *The Insider's Guide to Becoming a Yacht Stewardess: Confessions From My Years Afloat With the Rich and Famous* by Julie Perry

- *Working On Yachts and Superyachts* by Jennifer Errico

Appendix B
Nautical Terminology

Nautical Terminology

There are a many things you will be expected to know about terminology onboard. Your captain, first mate, and the head of your department will work with you on what you need to know. You will have to understand the common terms for different parts of the vessel. Below is a list of location names and a diagram that shows the colors of the lights that designate each area of the vessel. Port and starboard refer to the left and right sides of the boat, if you are facing forward towards the bow.

Terms	Light	Location
Port	Red	Left
Starboard	Green	Right
Stern	White	Aft
Bow	Anchor Light/White	Fore

Part of your responsibility will be standing watch while the boat is underway. It is important that you learn the basic safe navigation rules. At the very minimum you should know:

LIGHTS help us recognize situations at night. They tell us where the boat is, how big it is and which way it's moving.

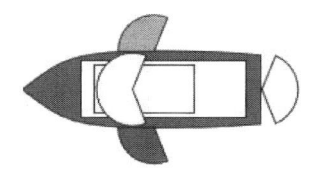

SHAPES help us recognize situations during the day.

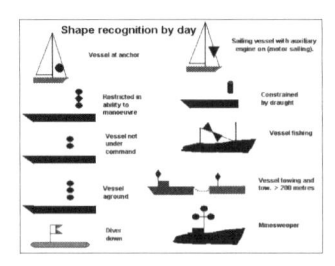

SOUNDS

Every vessel is required to carry some kind of efficient sound producing device to signal their intentions as outlined below. Vessels are required to sound signals any time that they are in close quarters and risk of collision exists.

- The term "**short blast**" means a blast of about one second.
- The term "**prolonged blast**" means a blast off from four to six seconds.

The following signals are the only ones to be used to signal a vessel's intentions (inland rules only).

- One short blast - I intend to change course to starboard.
- Two short blasts - I intend to change course to port.
- Three short blasts - I am operating astern propulsion (backing up).
- Five or more short and rapid blasts - Danger or doubt signal (I don't understand your intent)

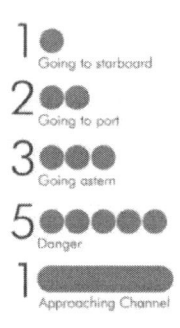

For More information Read: The USCG US Aids to Navigation System

http://www.uscgboating.org/assets/1/workflow_staging/Publications/486.
PDF

Basic Knots

You should know or have someone show you how to tie these basic knots.

- Bowline
- Square knot
- Clove Hitch
- Figure 8

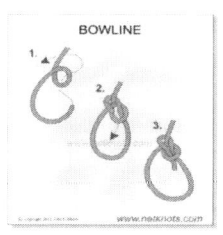

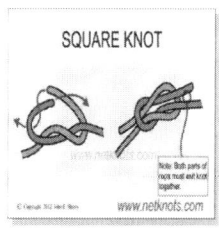

187

Additional Nautical Terms to Know

Terms		
LOA	Length Overall	Distance bow to stern
Draft	Depth from waterline to the lowest point	This is how deep the vessel sits in the water when loaded with bunker
Water line	Painted line on the hull	Line that is painted to show where water comes onto the hull. It shows how much water the boat displaces
Hull	Main Structure	The part of the boat that is floating in the water
Upper decks	Superstructure	The area above the hull of the boat. Main deck and up. The main deck will probably have a galley, a dining room, a main salon, an aft deck seating area, dayhead(s), and possibly Master cabin
Bridge Deck	Wheelhouse or pilothouse	The area above the main deck of the boat. May have a "sky lounge" or guest cabin. The captain's cabin, office, and chart room are probably on this deck
Lower decks	Area inside the hull	Areas below the main deck, in the hull. The crew cabins and crew mess area will be forward, and guest cabins will be aft. The engine room will be belowdecks

Diagram of power vessel

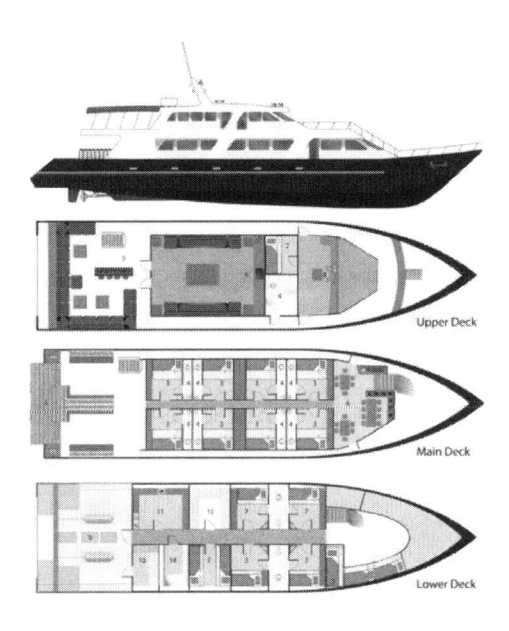

[www.slamdivers.com]

Diagrams of Sailing Vessel

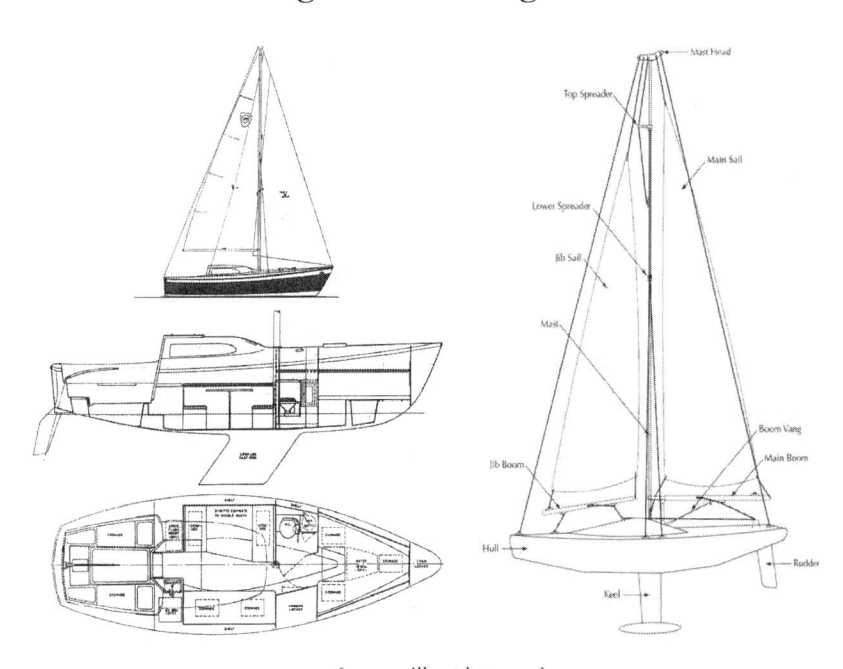

[www.sailboatdata.com]

Terms the Interior Crew Should Know

Side Gangway	Boarding Ladder to be used when boat is docked side-to
Passarelle	Hydraulic gangway that is normally used when the boat is docked stern-to
Transom	Stern surface area of a vessel
Winch	Device that winds in lines or cables
Fenders	Inflatable or impact absorbing material objects that hang between the boat and the dock to protect the vessel from touching the dock or pilings. Never refer to them as "bumpers"
Fender hooks	The hooks that secure the finders to the rail of the vessel
Rub rail	Protects the protruding hull area from damage
Chafing gear	A canvas or leather covering the fits around a line and protects the line from chafing and scratching the vessel
Heaving Line	A light line that is heaved to someone ashore to pull in heavier lines
Monkey's fist	A type of weight attached to the heaving line. A particular type of ball-knot is used to make a monkeys fist
Cleat	Object used to tie up small lines onboard
Tender	Small boat that is carried onboard
Davit	Hydraulic crane that is used to maneuver objects, such as the tender, on and off the vessel
Toys	Play items carried on board: wave runners, kayaks, slides, surf boards, etc.
Locker	Interior or exterior "closet" storage area
Hatch	Opening for access to another area; lifts up out of floor or deck

Terms That Are a Standard Part of Yacht Interior Domain

Main Salon	Guest common area similar to a "living room"; located on the main deck.
Dining Salon	Separate dining area onboard. Sometimes the main salon and the dining area are part of the same space. They may be separated by some type of room divider. Located on the main deck
Aft Deck Dining Table	Table on the deck immediately aft (behind) of the main salon, on the main deck
Master Cabin	Owner or Principal charter guest's cabin. Located on main or upper deck; larger and more luxurious than the other guest rooms
VIP cabin	Cabin for "VIP" guests; usually larger than other guest cabins, but not as large as the Master cabin
Galley	Area where food is prepared for guests and crew. There may be more than one onboard. Located on main deck or lower deck
Lounge	A bar or sitting area where guests can relax, watch TV, play video games, read, etc. Located on main or upper deck (where it may be called the Sky Lounge)
Staterooms/ Cabins	Guest rooms located on lower deck
Companion-way	Stairwell area leading from one deck to another
Porthole	Opening "window" in ship's hull. Normally round, and opens to let in air
Port light	Not a light at all. Non-opening round port or "window"
Deadlights	Storm covers for portholes and portlights
Head	Bathroom; one or more in each cabin
Dayhead	Bathroom located near guest common areas.
Head liner	Ceiling material
Bulkhead	Main upright walls within the vessel
Crew area	Crew mess and crew cabins located on lower decks
Captain's cabin	Located on bridge deck or lower deck

Bridge/bridge deck	The "bridge" refers to the part of the vessel the boat is operated from. Also called the wheelhouse. Located on the upper deck
Radio/chart room	Located on bridge/upper deck
Flybridge	Multi-use open deck above the bridge; may have navigation controls
Bilge	Lower innermost part of the vessel, below the waterline. Also used to refer to the water that collects in the bilges, which must be removed using a bilge pump
Water tanks	Hold fresh water
Fuel tanks	Hold fuel in reserve
Gray water tanks	Collect waste water from sinks, showers, drains, etc
Black water tanks	Collect sewage from toilets
Ballast	Material used to provide stability to a structure. Empty or full tanks can affect the stability of the ship. Ballast may be redistributed to alter its affect on the movement of the vessel, i.e., transferring fuel

Sailing Terms

Boom	A horizontal metal or wooden spar that sails attach to. It helps control the angle and the shape of the sail
Mast	Tall, vertical spar that carries sails and booms. Provides support for the rigging of sails and resists compressive and bending forces
Main sail	Larger Sail aft of the mast
Jib sail	Smaller sail forward of the mast
Rigging halyards	Wires that support the mast
Stays	Wires that support the mast fore and aft
Lee-ward	Direction away from the wind
Windward	In the direction of the wind
Running lights	Navigation lights

You will be expected to help with fenders and lines when the boat comes into the dock. Ask the bosun or first mate to explain docking procedure to you. Be sure to follow all safety guidelines when helping out on deck. Fenders come in many shapes and sizes.

[Images courtesy of blog@savvyboater.com and www.qingdaoyongtai.com]

Tie a line off onto a cleat, either on the dock or on the boat:

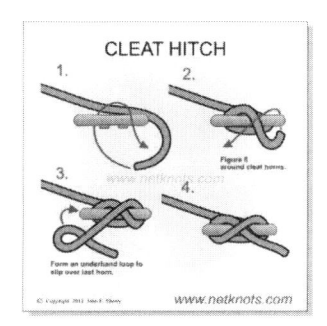

193

International Maritime Signal Flags

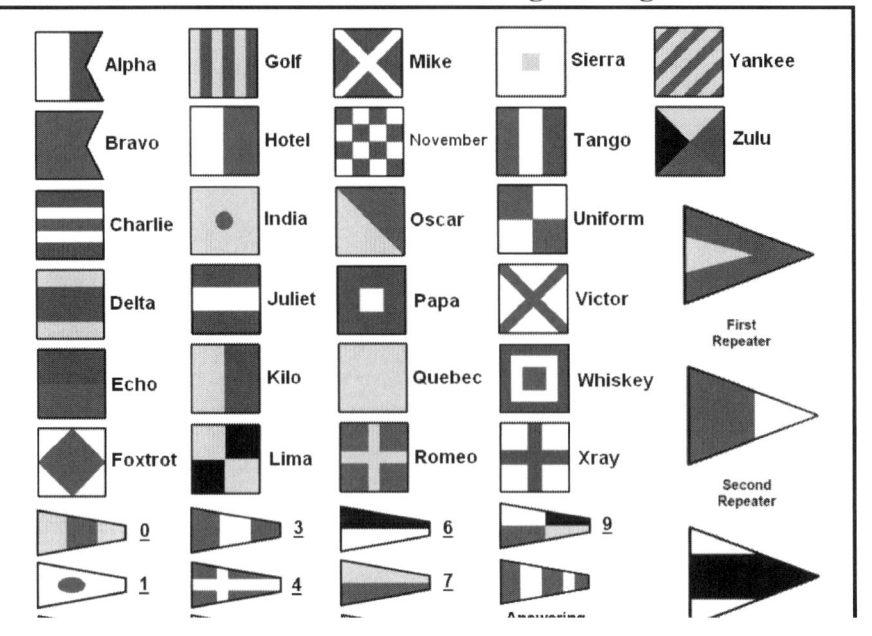

[Image courtesy of www.tattoospot.com]

International Distress Signals

Appendix C
Services Notes

A Summary of the Knowledge and Skills You Need for Service:

Personal Presentation
- Pride
- Care
- Confidence
- Attention to Detail
- Correct Uniform
- Importance of personal hygiene
- Importance of punctuality

Introduction to Service
- Definition of service
- Your role as a service provider

Food and Beverage Service
- Understand the different service styles
    - Plated Service/American Service
    - Silver Service/Russian Service/English Service
    - Other platter service-French Service/Butler Service
    - Synchronized Service
- Working with menus
- Mise en place
- Table setting and decorations
- Understanding the following services:
    - Breakfast, lunch, and dinner
    - Table service
    - Hors d'oeuvres/Canapés/Appetizers
    - Caviar Service
    - Buffet/Banquet service
    - Room Service
    - BBQ/Picnic
- Beverage service: Tea/Coffee/Wine/Cocktail/Water

Flower Arranging
- Flower presentation/table decoration

How to Make a Great First Impression

A favorable first impression is important. Guest and staff should be welcomed with courtesy and respect.

First Impressions: This is the order in which we gather information about a person upon first meeting him/her:

- Gender
- Skin color
- Height/weight
- Eye color
- Clothing
- Posture and Expression: Open, approachable, graceful and poised, confident, make good eye contact proper handshake
- Attitude: Positive, smiling, enthusiastic, interested, well-mannered, calm, respectful and courteous to all
- Presentation: Personal hygiene and good grooming, proper uniform (tidy hair, uniform, shoes, and nails), proper speech

Introductions: Introduce a less important or younger person to a more important one. Women rank higher than men, unless the man is a Royal. If Royal, than the order of introductions is: male to female and junior to senior.

Professionalism: It is important to be professional at ALL times.

- No discussion of crew problems or frustrations
- Strictly professional behavior that inspires confidence in guests.
- Loyalty to owner, guests, and fellow crewmembers
- No cell phones in front of guests.
- Be courteous, polite, gracious, and friendly.
- Keep a positive attitude.
- Avoid personal questions that may offend anyone.
- Do not use bad language in others company.
- No yawning, sneezing coughing or burping in front of others.

Yacht Stew Guru: Individual Guest Preference Sheet

Dates of Visits:	
Guest Name:	
Contact Info:	
Guest of/How Related:	

Allergies:	Notes:
Beverage Likes/Dislikes:	
Food Likes/Dislikes:	

Special Needs or Requests:

The Basic Knowledge of Fresh Flower Arranging

Mechanics to Keep the Flowers in Place:

- Floral foam, also called Oasis, comes in various shapes and sizes.
    - Green foam which is soaked in water
    - Brown foam which is used for dried flower arrangements.
- Pin holders or "frogs"
    - A simple frog has 4 prongs that point up
    - A pinholder is heavier and has a series of sharply pointed pins, designed to hold stems securely. Can be anchored with adhesive clay
- Wire mesh or wire netting (chicken wire): Can be used on its own or placed over floral foam to hold stems in place
- Adhesive tape: Waterproof tape used to secure wire, foam, and materials. Can be used to make a grid over the top of a vase
- Adhesive clay: Holds surfaces together
- Pebbles and marbles: Can be used as a design element as well as for securing stems
- Florist cone or tube: Can be used to hold single blossom

Equipment & Tools for Making Arrangements

- Buckets for holding and conditioning blooms
- Cut flower preservative—kills bacteria and provides food for stems
- Sharp knife for cutting floral foam, clay, removing foliage from flower stems, sloping cuts on stems, and vertical cuts in bottoms of stems
- Floral scissors—not suitable for cutting stems, because they crush them. May be used for cutting thin wire and other items.
- Secateurs—used to cut through thick or woody stems
- Watering can
- Wooden skewers—make holes in floral foam so stems are not damaged
- Mister—helps keep flowers looking fresh. Mist from the top down
- Turntable—great for all around arrangements

- Wire—support drooping stems, to bind blossoms together, etc. Different gauges:18-26 gauge/stub wire; rose wire is thinner, for finer work; reel wire comes wound on a spool
- Floral tape is a plastic or waxed paper tape used to cover stems. It binds to itself when warmed by the hands
- Candle holders—can be plastic or metal—use metal if candles are going to be lit

Waterproof Containers to Hold the Arrangement

- Vases, jugs, bowls, baskets, etc. that are waterproof or can have an insert to make them waterproof.
- Crystal vases are intended to hold flowers, but when using crystal containers for uses other than flower holding be sure to use a liner.

Other Items to Consider

- **Base**—Object placed between the flower container and the support on which it stands. Can be part of the design—to improve visual appeal and sense of balance
- **Accessories**—any non-plant materials to add decoration or accent…. stones, shells, coral, beads, pebbles, marbles, stones, etc.

Choosing Flowers and Plant Material

There are 3 basic types:

- Line Material or Outline Material—Tall stems, straight or curved, that set the frame of the arrangement
- Dominant Material—provides a center of interest. Bold flowers or foliage
- Filler Material—fills in bare areas. Covers the container, adds visual interest

Buy from a reputable supplier, and buy flowers at the right stage:

- Open stage is the best time to buy—each stem has a few open blooms and plenty of buds

- Bud stage—this it too early. Buds do not often open indoors
- Ripe stage—all flowers are fully open however the display will not last long

Pre-Conditioning and Conditioning Flowers

Pre-condition the following:

- Woody stems: Woody stems, tree blossoms, and large roses should have thorns removed and the bark scraped from the bottom of the stem. The end should be cut on the diagonal and then a vertical cut made up into the stem
- Milky Sap treatment: Some flowers emit a milky sap—poppies, ferns, daffodils, sunflowers, etc. The sap of some flowers can cause a reaction in other flowers which will lead to a shorter vase life and spoil your arrangement. If you purchase conditioned flowers from the florist you don't usually need to worry about this, as the sap flow will have ceased, but if you ever cut fresh flowers from the garden, it can be a problem for the first several hours after harvest. After conditioning, keep these separate from other flowers overnight to ensure that the fresh sap won't affect your arrangement. The sap also prevents stems from absorbing water. In this case, you may need to singe the bottom of the stem
- Spring bulbs—the white part of the stem cannot absorb water, so cut it off on a slant. This includes, tulips, hyacinths, and daffodils
- Wilted flowers—woody stemmed flowers such as roses that have wilted flowers and leaves can be covered with a paper bag and the bottom inch immersed in near boiling water for one minute to shock them back.
- Floppy stem—some flowers have stems that will wilt in the arrangement. To help support them in conditioning, wrap them in wet newspaper and stand them upright overnight. They may still wilt—floral wire may be used to stand them up.
- Large-leaves—should be rinsed to remove dust and soil, and then soaked in tepid water so that the tissues can fill with water.

Conditioning: Cut the stems on an angle to increase surface area. Deep immersion is optimal for most plants, but spring-flowering bulbs should be put in shallow water. Add floral preservative to a bucket of water and let flowers stand in cool dark place for 2-8 hours or overnight

Arrangement Styles

The most important element is harmony of design features.

There are 7 design features:

- Style, form, or shape. Is it a full-round arrangement, or will it have a flat back and face out?
    - A mass style has very little open space (example: the Beidermeier and bunch in a vase);
    - a line style uses line material to define the arrangement, and it has lots of open space (vertical, Ikebana, and abstract);
    - line-mass has a strong visual line but with more flowers and leaves to fill in the space (triangles, crescents, and Hogarth curve);
    - a miscellaneous style has elements of one or more styles (parallel, landscape, and miniatures).
- Color and lighting—take into consideration room décor, background colors, vases, etc.
- Proportion—the Golden Ratio is 1:1.5, meaning the height should be 1.5 times the measure of the width.
- Background and setting—style of a room, size of a room, colors in a room, color of background wall, height of dining table arrangements should all considered.
- Texture—a variety of textures adds visual interest
- Balance—is the arrangement top heavy, bottom heavy or balanced when you look at it?
- Movement or rhythm—does the eye tend to move from one part of the display to the next, is there a focal point or a center of interest?

Floral Arrangement Care

- Check water levels in vases daily and make sure floral foam is kept moist. Change the water in a vase if it becomes cloudy—this indicates bacteria.
- Protect from heat, drafts, and direct sunlight
- Keep away from fruit. It emits a gas which speeds up ripening of flower and they will not last as long
- Mist occasionally, spraying above and around the arrangement. Flower petals may be damaged by droplets. Mist more often if air is hot and dry

- Remove dead blooms from the arrangement
- Store your flower tools properly. Wash in soapy water, dry properly and store. Floral foam can be wrapped in plastic and be re-used, but use care here because it may contain bacteria.
- Make sure vases are clean and bacteria free before use. Use a flower preservative to kill bacteria and feed the flowers

Cut Flower Preservative Recipe #1

- 2 cups lemon-lime carbonated beverage (e.g., Sprite™ or 7-Up™)
- 1/2 teaspoon household chlorine bleach
- 2 cups warm water

Cut Flower Preservative Recipe #2

- 2 tablespoons fresh lemon juice
- 1 tablespoon sugar
- 1/2 teaspoon household chlorine bleach
- 1 quart warm water

Cut Flower Preservative Recipe #3

- 2 tablespoons white vinegar
- 2 tablespoons sugar
- 1/2 teaspoon household chlorine bleach
- 1 quart warm water

More Tips

- Trim away any foliage that falls below the water line. The wet leaves encourage microbial growth that can rot your flowers.
- Remove any unnecessary leaves because they will accelerate dehydration of the flowers.
- Flowers with milky latex-containing sap require special treatment. Examples of these flowers include poinsettia, heliotrope, hollyhock, euphorbia, and poppy. The sap is meant to prevent water loss by the stem, but in a cut flower it keeps the plant from absorbing water. You can prevent this problem by dipping the bottom tips (~1/2 inch) of the stems in boiling water for about 30 seconds or by flashing the tips of the stems with a lighter or other flame.

Appendix D
Housekeeping Basics & Overview

Yacht Stew Guru: General Housekeeping

The vessel's safety, integrity, and cleanliness are your responsibility. Here is an overview of what you need to know:

Boat-by-Boat: Be sure you're up to date on each vessel's individual requirements.

- Read manuals and info for your furnishings, finishes, and decorative items
- Follow manufacturer's instructions for using cleaning supplies. Test results for using new products by applying to an area that is not going to show, and use with care
- Have access to professionals for help and advice

Protect the Interior

- Materials onboard are expensive and likely to be more delicate than what you are used to at home
- You have different issues to deal with than in a home—salt in the air, exhaust in the air, humid environment and often extreme heat and humidity when in the shipyard
- Learn about the artwork and decorative items onboard, and the proper way to care for them. Know when to call in an expert or an art conservator. Know about any insurance requirements before you remove anything from the vessel. Know how to protect artwork.
- Take care to not damage finishes and surfaces
- Know your materials and be sure you understand any and all special requirements

- Know your cleaning tools and supplies:
  - Many products are too strong or too abrasive
  - Use the proper amount and the proper strength/dilution. Less is more
- Work with hygiene in mind-do not cross-contaminate. Have a system using specific materials for specific areas. Wash separately and/or dispose of properly
- Use proper cloths and sponges for wiping up. Do not use guest towels for cleaning. Products will damage towels
- Learn how to use chemicals and cleaning supplies safely. Use safety and protective gear properly
- Know which areas of the vessel you are required to care for- which rooms, fixtures (heads, showers, drains, laundry equipment, appliances, etc.).
- Pantry appliances—blenders, juice machines, coffee equipment
- Refrigeration—ice machines, wine coolers, refrigerators
- Cleaning equipment-vacuums, steamers, carpet cleaning equip
- What filters and ventilation you are in charge of-a/c filters; dryers and lint removal;
- Electronics and electrical equipment

Inventories and Purchasing

- Inventories and checklists of cleaning products
- Purchases
- Organization & reorganization
- Stowing items
- Organizing and re-organizing lockers, cupboards, and cabinets

Cleaning and detailing

- Always protect the areas where you are cleaning
- Have all of the proper materials on hand when you begin
- Different levels of cleaning: daily and detail cleaning. Detail cleaning is deeper cleaning
- Spray cleaning supplies onto your cleaning cloths, not onto the surface you are cleaning to avoid damaging other surfaces in the vicinity
- Sprays are for "cosmetic" cleaning, not for deep cleaning.
- Aerosol sprays have a propellant that is unhealthy

- Detail cleaning will be cleaning with great care, using tools to clean, polish, wax, and buff surfaces

Know Your Finishes

- Glass and windows
- Different wood finishes
    - Varnish-gloss or satin
    - Polished or waxed surfaces
    - Oiled surfaces
    - Painted or lacquered
    - Veneers--the surface is actually a very thin layer glued on
- Marble and stone
    - No strong cleaning products
    - No abrasive cleaners
    - pH neutral soap
- Metals-know whether you can polish it or not
    - Is it lacquered or coated
    - what type of metal is it--is it plated or solid
    - Stainless steel fixtures and fittings--is it brushed or polished

Taking Care of China, Crystal, and Flatware

- What kind of dishes do you have?
- Is it dishwasher safe? Usually heat damages surfaces
- Regular glass and crystal stemware
- Plastic and acrylic glasses
- Drying glasses properly
- Polishing glasses

Soft goods

- Carpets
- Upholstery & cushions
- Draperies
- Bedding
- Table linens

Cleaning Room By Room

- Bathrooms
- Staterooms
- Dining areas
- Lounge, entertainment, and common areas
- Crew areas
- Captain's cabin
- Cleaning routines and schedules with guests onboard, being discrete and "invisible"

Making beds and turndown service

- How often do you change sheets
- What is the design/routine for bedding and linens at night and during the day
- What is the routine for turndown--what do you do, what lighting settings, what treats are put out, etc.
- What is the laundry routine

Laundry

- Laundry symbols for Washing and Drying
- Maintaining and organizing laundry area
- Detergents and additives
- Bleach-hydrogen peroxide or Oxy clean are oxygen bleach, safer than chlorine bleach
- Fabric softeners liquid and sheets- are not good to use on fabrics all the time
- Stain removal products
- Tools and materials to have on hand for machine washing and hand washing

Washing procedures

- Machine wash
- Hand wash
- Dry clean

Drying techniques

- Machine dryer
- Air dry
- Flat dry

Ironing

- Know your equipment-hand iron or rotary iron
- Know your fabrics
- Know your techniques
- Know your folds

Valet services

- Packing and unpacking suitcases
- Clothing and wardrobe maintenance
- Shoe and leather care
- Toiletries and over-the-counter medicines

Other items to consider:

- Guest departure/ checklist for cleaning all areas of boat in timely manner once guests have left after a trip--what gets done first, how long it will take to get all areas put back together
- Turn-around time/ swapping out owners' belongings
- Preparing to go to sea/ check with Captain for info on how rough it will be and what needs to be stowed

Ironing Tips and Methods

The following section is courtesy of *Home Comforts* by Cheryl Mendelson.

What to Iron:

- Untreated cotton and linen woven fabrics almost always need ironing to look their best
- Tablecloths, napkins, curtains and other decorative pieces do not look good without ironing

What Not to Iron:

- Terry cloth towels and washcloths
- Comforters of other filled objects
- Stretch athletic wear
- Seersucker
- Pile fabrics such as velvet and chenille
- Do not iron clothes that have been worn, because it sets in the dirt and makes it harder to remove

Sprinkling/Spraying clothes and linens to dampen them:

- Permanent press and synthetic fabrics sometimes iron well when dry, and if not a steam iron is usually all that is needed
- Untreated cottons, rayons, and silks must be slightly damp to iron out properly. Linen should feel even more damp
- The easiest way to get things evenly damp enough is to remove them from the dryer or clothesline at the correct stage
- Dampening clothing allows the moisture to spread evenly and uniformly. Fabrics can be dampened the night before and then rolled and sealed into a tightly closed plastic bag or somewhere cool enough to prevent mildew to form. Linen should be damper than cotton.

Ironing Temperatures: The international symbols for ironing temperatures consist of one, two, and three dots:

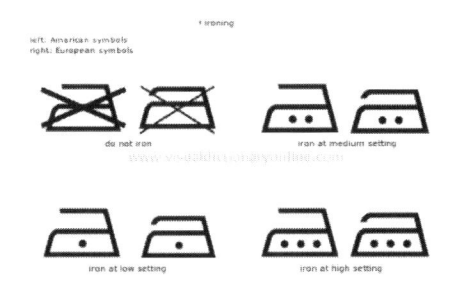

- One dot: cool (low temperature--248 degrees F; 120 degrees C), synthetics
- Two dots: warm (medium temperature--320 degrees F; 160 degrees C), silk and wool
- Three dots: hot (high temperature--370 degrees f; 210 degrees C), cotton and linen

Ironing Techniques

The terms *ironing* and *pressing* are often used interchangeably, but they are different things:

- Ironing: Sliding the iron back and forth over the cloth
- Pressing: Pressing the iron in one spot and then lifting the iron
    - Used to avoid crushing the cloth, giving it shine, or stretching or scorching it
    - Done partly by not sliding the iron and partly by using a "pressing cloth"
    - Press on the wrong side as much as possible
    - Wool: put a heavy, non-bleeding towel under the garment to prevent seams and folds from leaving imprints on garment surface
        - Wool will develop a shine if ironed on the front side
        - Lift the iron after each pressing. Do not go back and forth or you will stretch the fabric
        - Iron in the direction of the weave

209

- Silk ties: press on the back side.
    - Lay thick ties on a terry cloth towel
    - Place a pressing cloth over the tie
    - If wrinkles do not come out place a damp pressing cloth over the dry one

General Ironing Strategies

- Place article on ironing board and smooth it out. One hand works smoothing the garment and pulling it taut while the other works the iron
- When you put down the iron stand it on its heel or place on a non-flammable stand
- Begin ironing with the lowest temperatures and end with the highest temperatures last
- Keep a spray bottle or sprinkle bottle or clean, damp sponge handy
- Spray starch and spray sizing should be kept at hand
    - May starch only collars, plackets and cuffs plus fronts. Use more starch on these areas and less on others
    - May want to turn down the heat because starch is easy to scorch
- Collars and cuffs should be folded down and softly creased by hand
- To avoid shine, iron on the wrong side or use a pressing cloth
- Iron around buttons, hooks, snaps and zippers; never iron over them. Buttons may crack and metal objects may scratch the soleplate of the iron
- Iron embroidered or sequined cloths on a heavy towel to keep patterns raised and prevent cracking of sequins
- Use a pressing cloth when ironing lace and cutwork to prevent accidentally tearing the cloth
- Never iron the pile of a fabric. To steam a pile fabric, place on a heavy towel and hold iron a fraction of an inch above the surface.
- Steam ironing-
    - Use the proper steam level for the fiber.
    - Use the most steam for linen, the least for synthetics
    - Use the steam button to eject a steam spray on cuffs, collars, and other thick places

- Airing and ironing
    - It is a general rule that you iron things until they are dry and smooth, but not bone-dry. This prevents them developing a faint and unpleasant odor or mildew.
    - Over ironing may scorch fabrics, cause yellowing, or melt synthetics
    - Airing carries off the excess moisture without the dangers of over ironing
    - If you don't air them properly they are likely to carry dampness into closets

Ironing clothes: three basic rules

- Iron all parts that have double thickness--ties, bows, collars, cuffs, sleeves, pockets, etc
- Iron non-flat portions like ruffles, shoulders, and puffed sleeves before flat portions
- Iron the top before the bottom parts

Ironing flatwork

- Make certain that any items that will reach the floor are protected by clean sheet or tablecloth

Ironing linen

- Linen should be quite damp
- Ironing on the wrong side will prevent a sheen from developing
- On damask and other light-colored linens a sheen is desirable
- Hang ironed linen cloths while they still retain a hint of dampness at the seams or hems and then air dry
- Good linen tablecloths and napkins stay crisp without starch; fancy napkin folds require starch

Table Linens

- Round tablecloths- begin at the center and work out
- Table napkins- iron flat and do not iron in the crease
- Damasks are supposed to look glossy. They are ironed on both sides, wrong side first
- Linen is brittle, especially when dry, so take special care to be sure that crease lines are not ironed dry and the you iron along the crease line gently
- If it will be some time before tablecloths are used it is best for them to be stored unstarched and unironed

Ironing Sheets

Like it or not, ironing sheets is a part of your life. Here are some tips to make it easier. There are 2 basic methods:

- Long method: Using this method you can either iron both sides of the sheet, or only the right side. To iron only one side: Fold the sheet in half crosswise—bottom to top, wrong sides together and iron on both (right) sides. Or, if you are going to iron on both sides: first fold in half crosswise/ bottom to top right sides together. You would be ironing the wrong side first. Next, refold it wrong sides together and iron on both (right) sides. Keep folding crosswise/bottom to top and ironing as you go until you have created eighth folds. Then fold lengthwise, selvage to selvage. (The selvage is the side of the sheet.) Fold lengthwise again so you have folded selvage to selvage twice.
- Short method: Fold in half crosswise/bottom to top, iron once, and then fold as above.
- Abbreviated method: Fold in half crosswise (hem to hem) . Iron the bottom hem. selvage edges, and 18 inches of the top hem. Fold as above.
- Ironing fitted sheets: You have two choices: You can iron the fitted corners by stretching over the end of the board. Or you can leave the fitted corners unironed and iron only the flat part.

Starches and Sizings

Starches are plant starches. They are usually made of cornstarch and are used to stiffen; to add crispness, body, and glossiness; to make ironing easier; and to promote soil resistance--particles adhere less easily to smooth starched surfaces. Starches are best used on natural fibers. It is a good idea to use starch when you want extra body or stiffness on collars, cuffs, shirt fronts and on napkins for fancy napkin folds. There are different kinds of starch that give different finishes, such as Regular, Professional Finish, Heavy Finish, etc. There is liquid starch that you can add to the final rinse of the wash, and there are spray starches that you apply as iron. You can starch by hand in a basin of water. Be sure to measure correctly whenever using liquid starch.

Sizings are lighter. They are usually made of a derivative of cotton that dries and stiffens when it is heated. It is softer than starch and irons at lower temperatures, so it is best for fabrics that need to be ironed at lower temperatures. They are available in different finishes, too. The companies that make sizing also make Wrinkle Release products. You can make your own sizing with unflavored gelatin—one packet to 2 quarts of hot water. This is good for small pieces that need gentle stiffening. Dip the piece in and get uniformly wet. Allow to dry and then iron.

Cleaning and Maintaining Irons

Most irons these days have a nonstick soleplate and can be cleaned by wiping with a damp cloth when the iron is cold. Do not use anything abrasive to clean the surface of the iron because you will scratch it. There are products available for cleaning the surface of the iron. Sometimes you can clean it by making a paste of baking soda and water. Use an old, soft toothbrush to apply the paste to a cool iron surface. Let it sit for a few minutes and then scrub vigorously. This may be a little abrasive but if used occasionally should not be a problem. Try to clean the iron as you go, the longer it sits the harder it is to clean.

Some manufacturers require you to use tap water in steam irons and some ask you to use distilled water. Be sure that you know what kind of water you should be using in your iron. If your iron frequently becomes clogged, you may be using the wrong kind of water. Many new irons have a self-unclogging feature. If your iron becomes clogged, you can pour white vinegar into the water tank and, turn it on, let it steam for a few minutes. Iron a clean cloth to get the deposits out of the iron and let the iron cool, and empty the tank. Refill with cool water and drain to rinse it before you use it again. There are also commercial products you can buy for this purpose, but they are extremely caustic.

Cleaning Common Wood Finishes

Common Wood finishes

- Lacquer – A clear water or solvent based finish that creates a hard, durable, and flexible coating. Dries quickly so less chance that airborne particles get caught in the finish. Term also applies to the technique of applying multiple layers of varnish.
- Polyurethane – Water-or solvent based finish available in a range of sheens. It is a type of varnish that is made with a polyurethane resin. It is more protective and durable and helps protect against water and alcohol damage
- Varnish – A combination of oils and resin that produces a glossy finish. Slow-drying, which may allow dust and dirt to settle into the surface and damage the finish.
- Penetrating Oil – Coats the surface of the wood, seeps into the wood, and permeates the fibers. Tung, linseed, teak, Danish, and mineral oils are commonly used to finish furniture. They create a soft luster but do not protect as well as lacquer, polyurethane, or varnish.
- Shellac – A resin made from the secretions of the Coccus Lacca bug, which is indigenous to Thailand and India. French-polishing is a technique that was used in the 19th and early 20th centuries. It is achieved by applying successive thin coats of shellac and denatured alcohol.
- Paint – The practice of painting wood painting began to be done to make inexpensive pieces look valuable.. Early artisans used combinations of varnishes and powdered pigments to imitate Asian lacquered finishes. Often, a layer of plain varnish would be painted over the surface to protect the pieces.

Preventive Care of Wood Surfaces

- Protect from heat, light and humidity.
- Do not place near heat sources, such as warm air registers or fireplaces
- Wipe up spills immediately
- Use coasters for both cold and hot drinks
- Use placemats or tablecloths to protect surface before dining
- Place a protective mat or trivet under warm dishes to protect from heat
- Use a table pad under cloths to further protect the surface and to

insulate against sound.
- Place vases of flowers and potted plants on saucers
- Use felt or self-adhesive pads to protect from scratches by the underside of objects
- Store table leaves in the same environment as the table itself. Fluctuations in temperature and humidity can cause wood to shrink or swell.

Cleaning and Caring for Fine Art

Paintings

- Temperature and humidity: 18-19/Celsius, 55% humidity
- Type of glass: Mirogard Museum glass is treated to protect from UV light-should not use detergents of Windex
- Dust with soft cloth or clean with mild vinegar/water solution
- Do not spray solutions onto picture; it will eventually drip down underneath the matting and destroy the painting
- Art work is usually mounted on acid free paper or mat board
- Stretched canvas is easily distorted or torn
    - As it ages it becomes more vulnerable/brittle/easily damaged
    - Loses elasticity ad does not "spring back" as it once did
    - Relative humidity changes will cause it to tighten or sag

Frames

- Are usually custom made for each piece of art
- Should not be cleaned with solutions unless directed by conservator
- Patina on frame may be gold or silver leaf and easily removed
- Should be lightly dusted regularly to prevent dust and moisture from getting underneath
- Wood is constantly in flux and is affected by temperature and humidity

Glass

- Needs to be kept safe from accidental damage
- Wear white cotton gloves when handling glass

- Should be polished with lint free cloth and water with small amount of soap or alcohol polish
- Never use commercial glass cleaners on artwork
- Beware of heat build-up

Ceramics

- Glazed pottery is durable but easily damaged accidentally
- Decoration under the glaze are well-protected but may deteriorate form rubbing or scratching
- Dust with clean soft brush

Bronzes

- Highly susceptible to moisture, salt, and other corrosion
- Chemical changes that take place on the surface may be natural aging or may be sudden deterioration
- Easily scratched by metal objects. Small bronzes especially susceptible to over washing and over polishing
- Dust with fine brush a few times per year and use a cotton covered cuticle stick to dislodge any soil
- Never use water or detergent. Never polish any painted surfaces.
- May apply beeswax a few times per year

Appendix E
Yacht Stew Guru Assessments

A Guide to Assessing Chief Stews and Second Stew

Level I Knowledge: Junior Stew Assessment

Guest Relations and Etiquette:
- Greetings
- Forms of address
- Demeanor
- Punctuality
- Personal and Professional Boundaries
- Manners and behavior around guests
- Manners and behavior in service
- Cultural differences and conduct adjustments
- Religious and dietary preferences by nationality
- Proper health and hygiene
- Proper personal hygiene, health and organization in crew areas
- Proper uniform and personal presentation
  - Protocol for standing on deck and coming into and leaving port
  - Uniform and what it signifies to the individual, fellow crew members, owner, captain, and reputation of the yacht
- Duty rosters and scheduling for housekeeping, cleaning, and service
- Watch schedules and duties; standing orders underway

Administration:
- Job specifications and description
- Inventory requirements and procedure
- Various rosters for department
- Department procedures and guidelines
- Basic accounting and bookkeeping skills and software
- Basic to advanced computer skills and software
- Terms of contract
- Laws and regulations

Level II Knowledge: Second Stew Assessment

Transition from Junior to Mid-Level Position:

- Departments within the interior
- Guidelines on how to operate each department
- Establish your vision, mission and goals

Administration:

- Keeping inventories up to date
- Keeping your Service Guideline Book updated and relevant
- Keeping Housekeeping Guideline Book updated and relevant
- Keeping Laundry Guideline Book updated and relevant
- Effective use of checklists
- Department procedures
- Daily, weekly, monthly, and annual rosters

Interior Information Management System Maintenance:

- Contacts
- Records
- Schedules
- Standards
- Departmental Specifications

Etiquette Refresher:

- Cultural Differences
- Titles and forms of address

Food and Beverage:

- Understanding and ability to apply different service styles
    - Plated/American service
    - Silver Service/English or Russian Service
    - Other platter service: Butler/French Service
- Understand and be able to apply:
    - Caviar service

- hors d' Oeuvres/canapés/appetizers
  - Room Service
  - BBQ
  - Buffet/Banqueting service
  - Mise en place
  - Table setting and decorating
  - Breakfast, lunch and dinner
  - Napkin etiquette/ how to lay a napkin/tidy a napkin/replace a napkin
  - Clearing plates correctly
  - Beverage Service-tea/coffee/cocktails/wine/water

Housekeeping and Valet Service:

- Cabin day and evening service; turn down service
- Wardrobe Management
- Packing and unpacking
- Shoe care
- Cabin and public area cleaning methods
  - How to detail guest area
  - How to clean crew area
  - Checklists
  - Cleaning caddy
  - Having an eye for detail
  - Moving quickly and developing speed
- Yacht interior surfaces do's and don'ts
  - Wood/marble/ceramics/art and paintings
  - Mirrors/glass
  - Polishing metals
- Yacht interior fabrics do's and don'ts-different types
  - Bed linens, table linens, draperies and curtains, wall coverings, overhead coverings
  - Silks
  - Carpets
  - Suede/Leather
- Crew and Guest Laundry Procedures
  - Reading care labels
  - Spot treating
  - Care of uniforms
  - Professional ironing, folding, and presentation of articles of clothing

- How to treat linen/cotton/wool/silk/polyester and blends

Human Resources: Ability to understand HR procedure and guidelines within the department, including:
- Recruiting
- Training and Development
- Employee Relations
- Performance Management
- Compensation and benefits
- Regulatory compliance

Cigar Service: Understanding and ability to provide cigar service, including:
- History and production
- Storage
- Cutting
- Serving

House Plant Maintenance: Understanding and ability to store and handle fresh flowers and plants
- Storage onboard
- Cutting/Binding
- Presentation
- Maintenance

Level III Knowledge: Chief Stew Assessment

The Chief Stew should have all of Level II knowledge plus the following:

Management and Leadership: Monitor the vision, mission, and goals set by you via:
- Organizational Approach
- Planning
- Leading the team
- Delegating and controlling

Interior Administration:
- Create, implement, and manage all documents, Guideline Books, Checklists and Procedural Info
- Create, implement, and manage all interior information systems

Interior Financial Planning:
- Create, implement, and manage all budgetary planning, forecasting, and cost analysis
- Plan and prepare budget for all events
- Wages
- Petty cash

Food and Beverage Services: Understand and manage all food and beverage service styles.
- All of the above plus all tableside presentations of:
  - Gueridon Service
  - Filleting
  - Carving
- Synchronized service

Housekeeping and Valet Services: Ability to manage all aspects of housekeeping and valet services as listed above

Human Resource Services: Ability to understand, implement, and manage HR procedures and guidelines, including:
- Recruiting
- Learning and development
- Crew relations
- Performance evaluation and management
- Compensation and benefits
- Compliance

Event and Destination Services: Ability to provide and manage event services onboard and ashore, including:
- BBQ/Picnic
- Classic cocktail party

- Themed parties
- Dinner Parties

Ability to provide and manage destination services ashore, including:
- Shopping assistance
- Children's chaperone
- Owner's support during the day and evening

Flower and Plant Maintenance and Management:

- Purchasing/ordering
- Presentation and management

Appendix F
Sample Daily, Weekly, and Monthly Schedules & Tasks for Stews

The following is an overview of samples of several different daily, weekly, and monthly project sheets for common Stew responsibilities.

Daily Tasks and Projects
Date: _____

Special Assignments/Notes	Name	Any Notes	Date/ Check off
Lights, Flags, Opening Duties			
Clean Crew Mess & Stock Fridges			
Clean Captain's Cabin			
Check all refrigerators & Ice Machines			
Maintain Laundry			
Begin Task List			
Check Vital Inventories Throughout Day			
Set Up For Crew Lunch and Clear			
Set Up For Crew Dinner and Clear			
Closing Duties, Flags, Watch Duties			

Signature: _____

Monthly Tasks and Projects

Date: _____

Assignment	Name	Date Assigned	Date Due
Clean air conditioning vents in all cabins			
Maintain Vacuum Cleaners			
Maintain Washing Machines and Filters			
Maintain Dryers and Vents			
Maintain Irons			
Maintain Coffee Machines			
Maintain Refrigerators and Ice Machines			
Maintain Microwaves			
Maintain Dishwashers and Garbage Disposals			
Maintain Materials & Surfaces			

Signature: _____

Sample Schedule for 4 Stews

Chief Stew 6:30 am	Service Stew 7:30 am	Housekeeping 9am	Laundry Stew 8 am
Start laundry Set up breakfast table Start coffee, tea, etc. Tidy up salon, restock snacks and drinks	Squeeze juice Assist with breakfast set-up Check day heads Tidy bar, bridge, salon	Begin cabin duties as soon as guests are up When finished assist service stew with clearing and tidying as needed	Prepare beach bags with towels, sunscreen, hats. Prep for drinks and snacks Tidy crew areas, restock fridges; laundry, ironing, etc.
Serve and clear breakfast Set up for lunch Serve lunch	Stock fridges Assist with clearing bkfst. Assist with lunch & clearing; stay in service	Look after guests while service stew on break	Set up for crew meals; Guest laundry to be finished by end of day; Restock guest fridges
Break 2-4	Break 3-5	Break 4-6	Break 4-6
Guest service Afternoon tea/snacks Begin dinner preparations Serve dinner, clear, server tea/coffee	Set up for cocktails Assist with dinner set-up and service Serve dinner, clear, server tea/coffee	Dinner-relieve service girls for meal breaks Assist with guests as needed Assist in galley	Continue with laundry and ironing Be on standby to assist with service Assist with turndowns
Start breakfast set-up once dinner is cleared and dishes put away	Remain in service		
Check status of all stews Check menu with chef Retire by 10/10:30	Lights off, doors locked, guest areas tidy.	Retire by 10/10:30	Retire by 10:00
	Retire when guests have gone to bed		

225

Sample Schedule with 2 Stews On Board

	EARLY STEW/Service Stew	LATE STEW/Housekeeping Stew
7:30 Or earlier	Check/start laundry. Set up for breakfast. On many yachts guests prefer to be served outside if weather permits.	
8:00	Follow checklist for setting up breakfast service. By 8:00 table should be set. Complete everything in guest service area before anyone gets up. For example: Decaf and regular coffee ready, fresh OJ, butter and jams, cream cheese, cereal. Set up service station near dining area. Take plates, platters, and bowls to chef.	Late person should be on deck as hours of rest permit. If you cannot start cabin service, clean and guest areas that are open. For example, if guests are dining outdoors, work on cleaning main salon, skylounge, pilothouse and powder rooms. Begin cabin service as guests come up. Clean master cabin first if possible. Help others as needed. Continue to work on laundry and ironing. Check off items on checklist as you go.
11:30	Continue guest service. Service Stew to organize all items for lunch. Consult your checklist-- choose decor and set table, pull plates for chef, etc.	Check with service stew and chef to see if any help needed. Help with lunch set-up if needed. Continue laundry, cleaning cabins and guest areas.
12:00	Lunch for crew; stews to switch out as able.	
1:00-3:00	Serve lunch for guests at time specified or whenever they are ready. Both stews available to assist with service and cleanup as needed. Start breaks as time allows. 2 hours each stew. Early stew takes first break.	Maintain guest service and laundry while first stew on break
3:30-4:00	Check cabins. Check any guest service updates that may have been made while first stew on break. Maintain guest service and Laundry.	2nd stew on break
5:00	Begin dinner table set-up. Consult with chef and pull all service pieces for cocktails and dinner.	Maintain laundry and housekeeping checklist. Assist service stew as needed. Consult with service stew and chef and help pull all service pieces for cocktails and dinner.
5:30	Crew dinner-early stew first	Maintain guest service and laundry
6:00	Change to evening uniforms. Prep for cocktail hour	Change to evening uniforms. Assist with cocktail service. Begin evening cabin service when able to.
7:30-8:30	Guest dinner begins. Both stews serve first course. Housekeeping stew to assist when called.	Both stews serve first course. Turn down beds, dry showers, detail heads, collect towels and all guest laundry. Assist with dinner as needed.
10-10:30	When dinner is finished, help with cleanup. Early stew retires first as hours of rest requires.	Maintain guest service and laundry. Pull items for breakfast set up. Unload dishwasher and take care of trash. Check with /captain to see if you are to stay up until last guests retire, as hours of rest requires.

Sample Schedule for Yacht Crew Cook

Everyday
- Clean crew area after meals; watch person is responsible for dinner cleanup, tidy crew area, take out trash
- Check beverages stocked and keep crew fridge clean
- Make lunch and dinner
- Clean laundry room/ double check dryer filters
- Vacuum and/or wash all floors

Every Week
- Detail walk-ins and all refrigerators
- Clean galley, crew mess, laundry room, hallway walls
- Clean and inventory pantry shelves
- Detail clean stove
- Detail clean all galley areas
- Wash all trash cans
- Plan menus, make shopping lists and provision
- Add items to inventory

Once per month
- Check and maintain all air con filters
- Clean inside of all galley and crew cabinets
- Check and clean oven
- Clean vent in stove hood
- Check freezers and ice machines, defrost if needed
- Check and inventory cleaning supplies:
  o Diluted solution of vinegar and water on wood surfaces
  o Denatured alcohol on walls, overheads, all stainless
  o Lysol, Mr. Clean, or other general cleaner for floors and weekly on surfaces
  o Neutral pH soap, such as Ivory liquid, properly diluted with water to clean surfaces daily

Stew Daily Duties Without Guests Onboard:

Every day:
- Clean captain's cabin and office, wheelhouse and radio room
- Vacuum/dust all surfaces, kick plates, baseboards, air con vents, etc.
- Empty trash
- Use diluted vinegar and water on varnished surfaces
- Use alcohol/water on stainless; polish as needed
- Check all mirrors, glass, windows for smudges
- Vacuum carpet and/or canvas covers
- Wash floors
- Launder area rugs as needed

Throughout the day:
- Be available to welcome guests/contractors and off beverages at

Captain's request:
- Make sure interior surfaces are protected at all times, i.e. with contractors working or any projects that crew are involved with
- Check office at end of work day for any dishes or debris

Once Per Week:
- Clean and flush all toilets; Run faucets
- Check and replace light bulbs
- Dust all surfaces in rooms, including door tops, lamps, vases, windowsills, etc.
- Polish bronzes/ dust art pieces
- Check and dust or polish marble surfaces as needed
- Clean and organize all cabinets in stew pantry
- Clean and organize all cabinets in guest service areas

Once Per Month
- Check and clean all air con vents and filters
- Polish any stainless around doors, kick plates, etc.
- Dust/clean walls in all rooms
- Vacuum under sofa cushions
- Clean and organize linen lockers for supplies and turn-down items
- Clean, organize and inventory cleaning supply lockers and under sinks

As needed:
- Wipe out all guest drawers and closets
- Wash shower curtains
- Stock guest bathrooms

Master Stateroom:
- Clean and organize drawers, cabinets, and closets
- Inventory and organize toiletries
- Clean, maintain, and organize owner shoes, clothing and personal items

Miscellaneous:
- Organize and inventory light bulbs and batteries
- Check all electronics, touchpad's and remotes as needed
- Polish all silver, brass and other metal guest items
- Clean and organize all media, game, movie, and entertainment items
- Spot-clean or deep-clean carpet, upholstery, etc. as needed
- Work on projects list
- Polish all hardware, hinges, kick plates, interior stainless and metal fittings
- Clean and maintain all ice machines, vacuum cleaners, coffee machines, small electrical tools
- Inventory, clean, and stock all alcohol and wine items
- Maintain cleanliness of all items and surfaces in all stew areas and pantries
- Maintain all linens, table decorations, etc.

Duties without guests and underway:
- Meal service for crew
- Co-ordinate meal times and food items
- Check beverages for crew
- Put out snacks for watch duties
- Check boat every hour/ walk through all areas
- Assist with watch duties as needed if not on watch schedule
- Clean and check bridge area for cleanliness and clean as needed
- Follow rules for uniforms underway
- Follow rules for behavior underway/ notify bridge if you are going outside
- Help keep crew area tidy and quiet when watchmen are sleeping

DAILY
PROJECTS

Assignment/Notes	Name	Notes Addressed	Date/ Check off
Lights, Flags, Opening Duties			
Clean Crew Mess & Stock Fridges			
Clean Captain's Cabin			
Check all refrigerators & Ice Machines			
Maintain Laundry			
Begin Task List			
Check Vital Inventories Throughout Day			
Set Up For Crew Lunch and Clear			
Set Up For Crew Dinner and Clear			
Closing Duties, Flags, Watch Duties			

Sign Off: _____

MONTHLY
PROJECTS

Assignment	Name	Date Assigned	Date Due
Clean air conditioning vents in all cabins			
Maintain Vacuum Cleaners			
Maintain Washing Machines and Filters			
Maintain Dryers and Vents			
Maintain Irons			
Maintain Coffee Machines			
Maintain Refrigerators and Ice Machines			
Maintain Microwaves			
Maintain Dishwashers and Garbage Disposals			
Maintain Materials & Surfaces			

Sign Off: _____

Weekly Housekeeping Tasks

Month: _____

Cleaning tasks	Week 1	Week 2	Week 3	Week 4
Yacht Guest Areas	Check when completed	Check when completed	Check when completed	Check when completed
Dust all surfaces	☐	☐	☐	☐
Vacuum floors and baseboards	☐	☐	☐	☐
Clean floors	☐	☐	☐	☐
Wash windows and walls	☐	☐	☐	☐
Stew Pantry				
Wash the floor	☐	☐	☐	☐
Clean and disinfect countertops	☐	☐	☐	☐
Wash the cabinets, appliances (fridge, coffee machines, tea kettle, microwave, etc.)	☐	☐	☐	☐
Disinfect the sinks	☐	☐	☐	☐
Detail Dayheads				
Clean sinks, backsplashes and mirrors	☐	☐	☐	☐
Scrub the toilet	☐	☐	☐	☐
Wash the floor/launder rugs	☐	☐	☐	☐
Disinfect taps and polish	☐	☐	☐	☐
Clean wastebasket	☐	☐	☐	☐
Check & fill soap dispensers	☐	☐	☐	☐
Crew Cabins				
Dust and vacuum	☐	☐	☐	☐
Change sheets and wash bedding 2 x per week	☐	☐	☐	☐

Appendix G
Tips for Hiring a Stew

Every so often, I receive a request from someone who asks about my tips for hiring stews. First, I think an important consideration is whether or not the candidate fits into the culture of your organization. Each boat has its own unique personality, reflecting the tastes and lifestyle of the owners and guests as well as the yacht management style and the captain's wishes. The routine of service must be tailored and organized to meet the standards and expectations of the boat; and a job description that defines these standards and expectations must be given to the candidate as part of your process of assessing their suitability for the position.

Remember that you are looking for a service provider stew. The person providing service must have certain skills in order to meet the standards and expectations of the boat, including technical/housekeeping skills, service skills, ethics and protocol skills, communication skills, administrative skills, and people skills. Every stew has a particular service style and not every style suits every boat. So what would be the best fit for your boat? Frequently the owners and guests themselves would not be able to identify and describe the style of service they want. This is often determined by a method of trial and error, as they figure out over time what they don't want! Consequently, stews are often hired to correct past situations that they were not even involved in.

I always ask how many stews are required to complete the tasks that are necessary to meet the service expectations. A higher level of organization is needed to deliver higher levels of service, and thus more crew. Do the owners and guests want a formal meal setup for each meal, and do they prefer casual service or a combination of the two? The complexity of service skills required depends on how many courses will be served at each meal, the style of service desired, and how often the owners plan to entertain. Establish what level of wine knowledge is expected and other service considerations such as bar-tending, cognac and cigars, barista coffee skills, etc.

Always be sure to consider who the stews will be serving. In addition to owners and family, extended family, and former family, consider who will be on board as guests, and also their ages. Caring for small children, teenagers, elderly family members and/or pets requires different types of service and different amounts of time. Religious and cultural needs should also be taken into consideration, as well as planning and provisioning for holidays, birthdays and other social events. If the boat also provides charters, factor into the equation the amount of time between charters, whether or not the owners use the boat soon after a charter, and how much work is needed to switch from "charter" to "owner" mode.

Housekeeping and laundry are something else to think about. Depending on the number of guests and the number of crew that the stews are taking care of, laundry alone can take up the majority of every day. When the stews are expected to deliver valet services and care for very expensive clothing, shoes and other luxury items, it can be quite a challenge. Laundry facilities are often less than ideal and it takes a lot of technical skill to manage the crew's clothing while still maintaining appropriate standards for the owners' and guests' expensive belongings.

As for housekeeping, be sure to consider if the stews will be responsible for numerous pieces of valuable artwork and collectibles that must be maintained and protected. How elaborate are the cabin setups? Different fabrics and materials that are used throughout the yacht call for different standards of care: fine linens and silks require delicate care; ultra-suede requires frequent brushing; marble must be cared for meticulously; gold fixtures require gentle care. Having children on board can also considerably increase the level of upkeep.

Sometimes there are serious limitations in workspace and storage available for the stews to do their jobs. If the laundry room is no bigger than a closet, there will be problems carrying out these duties, and difficulties will have to be overcome. If there is no separate stew pantry to work out of, the chef and the stews will be sharing a common space. This can cause a lot of tension when the chef is trying to prepare crew and guest lunches at the same time as the stews are trying to finish, clear, and wash up the breakfast service for late risers.

Last but not least, are the crew themselves. Each boat has its own social structure and varying levels of cultural diversity. Will this new person fit in with the rest of the group? If they are emotionally mature, chances are they will know how to create balance in their lives and also be able to establish personal and professional boundaries. But often crew members have different levels of experience and hold different expectations about the performance of fellow crew members. The more experience one has, the easier it is to fit into a standard "role" and all that goes with it. Likewise, the easier it is to consider yourself an authority and thus be critical and impatient when others don't "measure up" to your expectations. That kind of power struggle can create a lot of tension.

So how do you know which stew to hire? First of all, you must come to a mutual understanding about the structure and personality of the yacht. Determine the preferences and lifestyle of the owners and guests, and consider the yacht's management style and the captain's wishes. Then you must decide who has the most in common with your vision of service and whether their style meets the level required to satisfy these expectations.

PRAISE

"Alene is extremely knowledgeable and has a natural gift for teaching, we are thrilled to have her as part of our faculty and as department head for our Yacht & Estate Service Arts Programs for new crew as well as experienced Chief Stews. This book will provide much-needed professional guidance and insight for every sector of luxury hospitality service."

Amy Beavers, Academic Principal, Maritime Professional Training - MPT, Fort Lauderdale

Printed in Great Britain
by Amazon